Negotiate
like a local

*7 Mindsets to increase
your success rate in
international business*

Jean-Pierre Coene
& Marc Jacobs

"Nothing is more practical than a good theory" (Kurt Lewin, 1890–1947). That may be so, but even a good theory may need some interpretation. This is precisely what Jean-Pierre Coene and Marc Jacobs have done. These two authors spent long careers in business, bumped into many problems, found that theory could help them, and have now put their learning into a comprehensive format. If you are an experienced salesperson, then you know that across borders, amazing and often frustrating surprises happen. This book will allow you to make sense of your experiences, and to reach better deals in the future. It uses, and interprets, the 6-dimensional model of national cultures developed by Geert Hofstede and others. That means it is based on solid ground, not hot air.

The book is eminently practical. It reads like a novel, using brief and clear summary of theory, well-chosen metaphors and a wealth of examples from real business life. Read it before establishing new contacts, and return to it when you wish to make sense of your experiences. I have no doubt that both you and your future business partners will benefit.

Gert Jan Hofstede

PUBLISHER

Hofstede Insights

Hofstede Insights
www.hofstede-insights.com
info@hofstede-insights.com

AUTHORS
Marc Jacobs
Jean-Pierre Coene

EDITOR
Daisy Radevsky

COORDINATION & FINAL EDITING

boooks·

Boooks by Sibylle Cosyn
www.boooks.eu

PRODUCTION
Amazon books
www.amazon.com

Copyright © 2017 by Jean-Pierre Coene and Marc Jacobs

ISBN 978-1976340130
First edition, first impression

We'd like to thank everyone who kindly contributed their ideas and their time. Their feedback has been immensely valuable.

Special thanks go to:

Linda Matthewman and Emily Jacobs for their support and patience.

Prof. David Arnold, Prof. Gert Jan Hofstede, Huib Wursten, Masato Oue, Patricia Ford, Nicolas Fries, Daisy Radevsky, Regis Heyberger, Philip Cashman, Naoya Gomi, Jean-Philippe Coene, Peter Stansby, Egbert Schram, Celia Zanin, Thomas Imfeld, Tatjana Von Bonkewitz and Angela Wang.

Index

Mindset 1: Negotiating with the 'Competitor' 47

Mindset 2: Negotiating with the 'Organiser' 65

Mindset 3: Negotiating with the 'Connected'   77

Mindset 4: Negotiating with the 'Diplomat'   87

Mindset 5: Negotiating with the 'Reciprocator' 101

Mindset 6: Negotiating with the 'Marathonian'   113

Mindset 7: Negotiating with the 'Craftsman' 129

The Science of Culture 141

Annexes

CHAPTER 1

Introduction

"What does a fish know about the water in which it swims all his life?"

— ALBERT EINSTEIN

Have you ever experienced an international deal going wrong and not understood why? Have you felt a buyer was being unfair or rude? Have you been confused about why negotiating was taking so long, or have you perhaps felt rushed?

You've taken all the courses, you understand how to develop business and how to close deals, but somehow, things are different once you're dealing with people from countries other than your own. The approach and style that made you very successful in your own country don't seem to work that well anymore.

At any of these points, have you thought about how culture might be affecting the challenges you face? Very likely, the reason is to be found in the cultural differences between your home country and the countries you are dealing with. In a world where business is becoming ever more global, the development of intercultural competence has become absolutely vital.

A couple of years ago, Marc was working on a deal with a major international company headquartered in the Netherlands. He was very close to finalising the last details when external circumstances required him to hand over the negotiation to one of his colleagues. François knew the customer and the details of the negotiation very well so Marc asked him to take over and close the deal. Marc was totally confident that François would be able to pull it off easily.

Several weeks later, François and Marc were catching up and Marc enquired about the status of that specific deal. François went quiet for a bit and then told Marc that he'd recently had a meeting with Bert, the Dutch Purchasing Director. He went on to say that from his perspective, the meeting had been an absolute disaster.

You can imagine Marc's shock upon hearing this news so he asked François to elaborate. "Well," François said, "Bert was extremely aggressive. I was so shocked by his behaviour that I can't possibly see how we can finalise the deal."

Marc was puzzled by this situation, especially because François had an excellent track record in dealing with various big accounts. As he was trying to understand what was going on, it dawned on him that François' experience and success had been exclusively with French customers.

Marc grew up in the north of Belgium, very close to the Dutch border and is used to dealing with his Dutch neighbours who have a reputation for being extremely direct.

As you may have guessed from his name, François is French and, in France, business negotiations are conducted in a rather diplomatic way. From a French perspective, the Dutch directness is considered very rude. Such a combative approach would only be used in France by someone trying to blow up the deal. However, from a Dutch perspective, direct communication is simply an efficient means to avoid misunderstandings. There is no connotation of rudeness whatsoever.

Now the situation had become clear to Marc. Bert had tried to paint a clear picture for François so that François would be able to analyse his needs and come back with the best possible solution for both companies. From Bert's perspective, there were no hidden agendas and no emotions attached whatsoever.

Marc explained to François that Bert's objective was to achieve a win-win situation and that he was convinced that if François took a more direct approach, the deal would be quickly and successfully concluded. From a Dutch perspective, a clear and transparent approach builds trust and creates a long-term partnership.

François felt very uncomfortable as it was an approach that felt wrong to him. Nevertheless, he took the advice and went back to see Bert.

A few days later, he called Marc and told him that, to his surprise, it had worked very well and he'd successfully finalised the deal in a short and very efficient meeting.

CHAPTER 2

Why this book? Who is it for? How should you use it?

Our aim is to provide you with a practical system based on a limited number of easily understandable mindsets that help you to negotiate successfully anywhere in the world.

You will learn which mindset is most prevalent in which country and how to adapt your approach to it.

During our careers in international business, we have learned to appreciate the importance of culture in our interactions with our customers, which is what ultimately led both of us to join Hofstede Insights. Hofstede Insights is a specialist consultancy in Intercultural Management and Organisational Culture with a mission to provide insights into the impact of culture. This book is built on Geert Hofstede's world-renowned 6D model of national cultures and Huib Wursten's concept of Culture Clusters™ (→ see chapter 3 and chapter 13).

We have found that there are some very good academic books [1] that take the impact of culture in international business into account, but very few books that have been written in an easy 'how to' format. With this book, we aim to fill that void and combine a solid academic framework with many years of experience in the field.

You can use this book in two different ways. If you use it as a manual to find out how to best conduct a negotiation in a specific situation, simply go to annexe 1: 'List of Countries', choose the country of interest and read the corresponding chapter.

If you would like to become truly competent, understand the finer nuances and have much of this knowledge at your fingertips, we recommend you read the whole book, so you understand the academic underpinning of our system.

We structured this book in a way that is culturally consistent with the preferences of a typical anglo-saxon reader. This means that we dive quite quickly into the 'how to' rather than first explaining the big picture and the academic underpinning of our approach. If you are like us and prefer to understand the 'why', the background and

---

1 An example of such a book is: 'International Business Negotiations' by Pervez N. Ghauri and Jean-Claude Usunier.

the academic underpinning before moving to the application, we recommend you start by reading chapter 13 and then come back to the beginning of the book.

As our earlier example shows, it is crucial to understand the difference between one's own cultural framework and that of one's negotiating counterpart. This is much harder than you may think. Generally, we are not even aware of our own cultural programming until we experience a culture shock by moving to a country where 'the way things are done around here' is substantially different from at home. Only then do we begin to realise the extent of the differences between our 'normal' and someone else's.

Whilst you are reading, always keep in mind that how you will interpret this book will depend on your own cultural perspective.

Jean-Pierre Coene & Marc Jacobs

Introduction to the 6D model[2]

2 Source for the description of the dimensions: www.hofstede-insights.com

3

Before diving into the core subject of the book, it is useful for you to have at least a superficial understanding of Hofstede's 6D model.

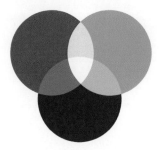

Most of you will be familiar with the RGB colour system used to define any colour on your computer screen. You can think of each individual colour (red, green and blue) as dimensions of colour with a scale from 0 to 255. Any colour is made up of a certain amount of red, a certain amount of green and a certain amount of blue.

Similarly, Hofstede's 6D model breaks down a national culture into six dimensions with a scale from 0 to 100. So just like one can describe any colour in three numbers, the 6D model can describe any national culture in six numbers (one on each of the six dimensions).

So what are these dimensions and what do they mean? Below you will find each of the six dimensions with their scientific names, as well as a short description of their practical implications. For a more detailed explanation, history of the model and the scientific background, have a look at chapter 8.

3.1 Power Distance Index (PDI) or attitude towards hierarchy

This dimension has major implications for the way a country (or institution or organisation) is structured and organised. In societies that have a low score on this dimension, one can say that hierarchy is there for convenience. It is not about power, delegation is natural, and people lower down in an organisation expect to be consulted, to take responsibility and to make decisions. The ideal leader is a facilitator who consults and coordinates.

On the opposite side of the spectrum, hierarchy is an expression of existential inequalities that are just part of life. Decision making is centralised and the rest of the organisation is expected to execute and not question. It is considered normal that the higher up in the organisation one is, the more special privileges one has. The ideal leader is autocratic.

3.2 Individualism versus Collectivism (IDV) or attitude towards groups

A society's score on this dimension is reflected by whether people's self-image is defined in terms of 'I' or 'we'. Communication tends to be more explicit and verbal in individualist countries, whereas in collectivist countries, reading between the lines (implicit or 'high context' communication) is the norm. In individualist societies, people tend to prioritise the successful execution of a task or a contract over developing and maintaining relationships. On the opposite end, in collectivist societies, developing and maintaining relationships come first and the successful execution of tasks comes second.

3.3 Masculinity versus Femininity (MAS) or attitude towards motivation[3]

Masculinity stands for a society in which social gender roles are clearly distinct: Men are supposed to be assertive, tough and focused on material success. Women are supposed to be more modest, tender and concerned with the quality of life. Society at large is more competitive. Status is obtained through success. In these societies, although it is more and more acceptable for women to be assertive, tough and focused on material success, it is generally NOT so much accepted for men to be modest, tender and concerned with quality of life.

---

[3] This topic warrants a 'health warning' as the wording 'Masculinity versus Femininity' is a potential source of controversy, especially in societies that score relatively high on this very scale. We decided to keep Hofstede's original description as we are not qualified to change this common and well-understood terminology in the social sciences. We would like to suggest to the readers that they can think of this dimension as 'tough' versus 'soft'. For further information, visit www.hofstede-insights.com.

Femininity stands for a society in which social gender roles overlap substantially. Both men and women are supposed to be modest, tender and concerned with the quality of life. These societies will tend to have strong social support networks, generous parental leave provisions for BOTH parents, strong social security systems, a 'work to live' ethic, etc. Very good examples are found in the Nordic countries.

3.4 Uncertainty Avoidance Index (UAI) or attitude towards uncertainty

Countries with a high uncertainty avoidance score maintain rigid codes of belief and behaviour and are intolerant of unorthodox behaviour and ideas. There is a need for rules and formality to structure life. Competence and expertise are highly valued and levels of anxiety tend to be higher. Societies with low uncertainty avoidance scores maintain a more relaxed attitude, in which practice counts more than principles. People in these societies tend to be more entrepreneurial and innovative.

3.5 Long Term Orientation (LTO) or attitude towards time

Societies who have low scores on this dimension generally prefer to maintain time-honoured traditions and norms, while viewing societal change with suspicion. In these societies, the 'truth' tends to be absolute, encouraging black and white thinking. Those with a culture which scores high, on the other hand, take a more flexible approach. The 'truth' tends to be less absolute and more context dependent. They encourage savings and efforts in modern education to prepare for the future.

3.6 Indulgence versus Restraint (IDV) or attitude towards happiness

A high indulgence score demonstrates a society that allows relatively free gratification of the basic and natural human drives related to enjoying life and having fun but also to being violent. A score on the restraint end of the scale shows a society that suppresses the gratification of needs and regulates it by means of strict social norms.

CHAPTER 4

The 6 Steps of the Sales Process

4

Those of you who have conducted commercial negotiations will know that there are multiple steps one must go through in order to close a deal. We will call this the 'sales process'. We have created a model of the sales process which consists of six distinct steps.

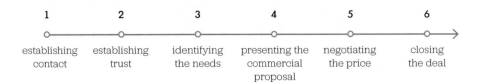

1	2	3	4	5	6
establishing contact	establishing trust	identifying the needs	presenting the commercial proposal	negotiating the price	closing the deal

These 6 steps are always present but depending on where in the world you are negotiating or the type of negotiator you are dealing with, the process will be either linear (Western approach) or more circular (Eastern approach). In the West, generally the steps will be followed in a sequential fashion whereas in the East, the order may not be the same, the distinction between the steps may be less clear and some of the steps may be revisited at any time.

4.1   Establishing contact

Any sales executive knows that this first step can be far harder than one might imagine. Making contact, getting that first meeting, is not always easy. The only two exceptions in any culture are: if you work for a highly prestigious company (say, Airbus, Boeing or Google), when, chances are, a meeting will be granted out of simple curiosity, or if you are a celebrity. If a retired tennis star such as Andre Agassi were to represent your competitor, he or she would likely find it far easier to obtain a meeting than you would…

But if you don't work for Google and you're not a retired tennis legend, then we're afraid you're in the club of those that need to work hard at prospecting for new customers. We will see that the degree of difficulty of this first step and the way to go about it are very different from culture to culture. In some cultures, a simple phone call is enough, in others you need to find a way to get yourself introduced by a trusted person, and in others again it's a matter of sheer persistence and you might even need to call ten times before you are able to breach the firewall.

This is where some of the magic of our profession lies. Non-sales people often wonder how we're able to enter those seemingly impenetrable fortresses. We have these innate but finely-honed senses which allow us to understand what makes others tick and what their needs are. We all have a personal approach and a charisma that is unique to us. This is how we do our jobs.

4.2   Establishing trust

Let's be frank. Most of us distrust who and what we don't know and that is perfectly natural. It is ingrained in us and makes sense from an evolutionary perspective. So it's only natural that you will have to put a lot of effort in to establishing trust.

Sometimes we forget about this step because it comes so naturally to us, but establishing trust, making sure we're on the same wavelength, showing we're on the same side, is essential. Whether you're selling a turnkey factory or a piece of software, you won't get anywhere unless you've established some basic common ground, some minimum level of trust with your customer. It is easier to establish this trust if you work for a large reputable company than if you work for a start-up, but you can do it either way. Let's not forget that to negotiate also means that you are providing a service to each other. Doing business has a degree of intimacy, and the buyer will appreciate it if you understand him mid-sentence. Anticipating his questions helps to establish a favourable atmosphere for good communication and a lasting business relationship. And it's not only the customer who needs to trust us – it's as important that we feel a reciprocal trust in them too.

   If you're negotiating a big contract, it is quite customary for many people to be involved on both sides. This makes establishing trust significantly more complicated and you will need to employ all your skills and senses to understand the relationships between the participants, and to know what to discuss with whom at what time. As a professional, you will automatically manage this competently within your own country.

   Knowing that each country has its own ways to establish trust, you can begin to imagine the intricacies and complexities of doing this internationally. We'll see that this step is crucial when working with different cultures because there is usually a quite natural distrust in both directions. This increases the challenges that need to be dealt with before a workable level of trust is established.

4.3   Identifying the needs

This step is not always formally identified, but it is obvious that you need to make sure both parties agree on what the needs are. Even when working within your own country, this can be a source of misunderstanding and must be undertaken with sufficient diligence and attention to detail.

   Knowing how challenging this step can be even within you own culture, you can imagine how different it can be in another. In some cultures, the process starts with a general introduction from the seller to make sure the buyer has a good overview of all the products, services and solutions the seller has to offer. The seller, therefore, can rest assured he's not missing an opportunity outside of the initial scope. This is a deductive approach, starting from the big, general picture and then homing in on the detail.

Other cultures can be quite the opposite and use a more inductive approach, where you may be presented with a clearly defined problem and asked to offer the best solution for that specific problem only. Such approach lends itself to completely de-humanised processes like automated 'RFQ's' (Request for Quotation), which are very prevalent in the Anglo-Saxon world.

In some cultures, (e.g. Asia and Latin-America), the human element is so important that the balance can be completely tipped by the person-to-person relationship between customer and supplier. The challenge presented to the supplier is, essentially: "We trust and like each other so what business can we do together?"

Throughout the world, you will find many variations in between these two extremes. Depending on how different your own culture is from your customer's, you may find it more or less difficult to accurately establish his or her true needs.

4.4   Presenting the commercial proposal

Now that the previous three steps have been successfully concluded, the time has come to present the commercial proposal. You may have drafted it already during the previous steps but the final price might not have been determined yet. If you're Belgian like us, you will experience this as the most delicate phase.

THE ARGUMENTS THAT MATTER
Sometimes, the product characteristics just aren't the sales arguments that matter. Your instincts will have taught you which arguments matter, and which are really the important ones for the buyer, in your own culture.

Let us give an example which we'll use again for each cluster, later on in the book. Imagine you're trying to convince a local distributor to buy (and resell) a limited edition, high-end wristwatch based on an entirely new concept. The following is a list of sales arguments you may think of when making your pitch:
· Reliability
· Elegance of the design
· Exclusivity of the watch (limited edition)
· Technical performance (e.g. precision of time-keeping or water-resistance)
· Good investment (keeps its value over time)

· The status it provides to the owner
· Environmentally friendly production

We will see that the choice of arguments, as well as the order in which you present them, is highly influenced by culture.

THE WRITTEN PROPOSAL

Even in today's age of email and the internet, many cultures still ascribe a high degree of importance to this document. It is a cornerstone of the play that is being enacted; a promise and a guarantee. It sums up all the conditions, exceptions, rebates, bonuses and the like and is signed by a manager or a director. It doesn't have to be on paper anymore and can take an electronic form. But the whole point is to have a reference document.

THE PRICE STRUCTURE

In order to illustrate the different ways cultures tend to structure pricing, let's use the example of a car.

On one end of the scale, we have the Anglo-Saxon countries where the price of a car is generally advertised on a big sign on top of the car. What is displayed is a single all-in price in as large a font as possible. The deal is simple and exceedingly clear without any room for misinterpretation or misrepresentation. What you see is what you get for one price.

On the other end of the scale, in some cultures you will find that same price presented, but described as that of a basic car, with a long list of separately priced optional extras, which are included in the price as 'free extras'. This is designed to convey a message to the buyer that he's getting a special deal.

We'll see that each culture has its own way of presenting a price and that what would be normal to you may not necessarily suit your customer.

THE PRICE

In Jean-Pierre's French-Latin culture, a well-managed sale is one where all the details have been agreed except for the price, which is the last hurdle. We will see that this is not so in others. It might even be the complete opposite.

His French-Latin culture, known for its high-handed intellectualism, doesn't like to talk about money. It is so pronounced that some classes of society will avoid socialising with 'mere sales people' who build their life around that vulgar topic of money, of price. This is very Latin behaviour; money is dirty. Ever since the time of the Romans, we've had to remind ourselves that money doesn't stink. The flip side of this is that the buyer tends to have a particular reputation in his company because he works with sellers (the devils!). He will have very precise instructions about which invitations and which presents he can accept.

MONEY IS DIRTY
In many cultures, particularly among the higher social classes, money is considered dirty. We advise you to take this into account early on in your analysis of your counterpart. Although all businesses in the world revolve around money, not all of them have money as the main objective. Growth, development, education and welfare are also profound motivations of a lot of businessmen, and money is considered as the 'nerf de la guerre' – the key element you need to achieve your ultimate goal.

4.5   Negotiating the price

Throughout the world, the definition of what constitutes a 'good price' varies tremendously from region to region.

In Jean-Pierre's culture, the price, although very important, is only one element of the deal. Often, it is the sales manager's job to make sure the buyer understands and appreciates the value of all the other elements that justify the price. Usually, the first price will be refused. The buyer has only done a good job when she has put the supplier under pressure. A game commences which we might call a 'diplomatic ballet', with many back and forths, during which the seller will change, improve and fine-tune his original offer. The importance of the ballet is directly proportional to the importance of the deal being negotiated. When the original offer was made, a plan B was prepared in parallel to allow the seller to quickly counter demands from the buyer. Obviously, a good buyer knows this, and so the dance begins. If the negotiation involves many participants, this can be a lengthy, drawn-out process during which the needs can be re-defined, cost prices recalculated and margins re-assessed. The quality of the sales manager, the degree of their preparation of the negotiation, and the success of the previous steps of the process will make a crucial difference.

During the initial steps of the process, it is important to find out who the decision maker is. Is it your counterpart? His or her boss? Is it a team? If so, what are the team dynamics, and who has the real power? This might be much less obvious than you think.

A PERSONAL ANECDOTE:
Marc was invited by a potential new German customer to participate in a technical qualification round, as they were planning to convert part of their portfolio to a new type of packaging. Their brand was built on the quality of their product and moving to this new packaging type was potentially a risky move. Marc received a phone call from the quality manager who told him that he was inviting all the players in the market to submit their best products for testing and proudly explained the test protocol he had devised. His requirements were

way beyond well beyond standard market specifications, but were achievable at a reasonable extra cost. Marc's team decided to go all out for the qualification round and came out squarely on top. Then the time for commercial negotiation came. Marc had gotten to know the quality manager quite well and it had become clear to him that because the company's brand was built on the quality of its products, he was a very powerful participant in any decision that might affect the brand. Germany is a country where experts are deferred to, probably more so than in any other country in the world. So even though they were moving into commercial territory, Marc knew it was unlikely that the purchasing manager of the company was going to decide anything contrary to the recommendation of the quality manager. Suffice to say it was one of his better pieces of business for a long time, and it was built on understanding the local culture and a correct identification of the real decision maker.

4.6   Closing the deal

THE IMPACT OF TIME

During this step, it is important to make constant progress. Too much non-action discourages everyone. The sales manager knows she must balance patience and efficiency. And sometimes it is better to withdraw completely.

THE FINAL DECISION

Imagine a very typical situation: you are in competition with several other suppliers and the buyer lets you know that, on the whole, you have the best offer. Is the deal done? Not by a long shot. You are close to the goal, but, as the English say, it isn't over until the fat lady sings. You may find that there are still people (top managers, a committee) that must approve the deal. How will this decision be made?

In Jean-Pierre's culture, there usually remains a bit of mystery, deliberately cultivated by the 'powers that be' at the top of an organisation. You may have the best offer, but the numbers, and even the price (which was very important during the negotiation), can become less important when it comes down to getting the deal signed on the dotted line. It is crucial to try and find out as early as possible what the real decision-making process is. Who really holds the power? Who are the real decision makers? Does your counterpart have a mandate? Are you sure you know all there is to know?

CHAPTER 5

The
7 Mindsets of
International
Negotiation

As we have said, our aim is to give you a practical system based on a limited number of easily understandable mindsets that help you negotiate successfully anywhere in the world.

You will learn which mindset generally is more prevalent in which country and why. That doesn't mean that this is always the case and it is up to you, as part of your first steps in the sales process, to identify which one of the seven mindsets best describes your counterpart. This will allow you to adapt your approach appropriately and maximise your chances of success. Just 15 – 30 minutes of focused attention and some targeted questions will allow you to determine your counterpart's cultural mindset.

By now, you may be thinking that condensing everyone in the world into seven cultural mindsets is too simplistic; that people are individuals and cannot be placed in boxes. We will demonstrate to you that our system, if applied appropriately, will allow you to be successful anywhere in the world. For each mindset, we will provide you with a list of countries. These are meant as a guideline only and will help you draw a mental picture of the mindset.

Huib Wursten, senior partner of Hofstede Insights, developed the concept of The 7 Culture Clusters[©4]. A culture cluster is a group of countries which share specific cultural characteristics based on the Hofstede 6D model[5]. Culture clusters group countries that have a similar view on the way society works and a similar idea of what is 'normal' for them.

The way people negotiate, the way customers behave, the way decisions are made, the way people are motivated and the way people convince are distinctly different between each of the clusters.

For each cluster, we have come up with a mental image which attempts to typify the mindset of the person you're likely to be dealing with. It is not intended as a fixed identity but rather a rough guideline.

Because it is difficult for anyone to see his own cultural framework clearly, you may want to have a look at www.hofstede-insights.com to find the scores for your own country or any other country you are interested in. You may feel that your country scores are not representative of you; you may have grown up in a multicultural environment or you may have lived in multiple countries during your formative years.

4   See chapter 13 for a detailed explanation of the Culture Clusters. Wursten developed his concept of the culture clusters at a time when Prof Hofstede had only identified the first 4 dimensions, PDI, IDV, MAS and UAI. For our purpose of international negotiation, whenever it is salient and provides additional insights, we will include the 5th dimension as well as the 6th dimension. Because there is a lot of ongoing academic research in the field of culture and especially around dimension 5 and 6, we may revisit this in a future edition.

5   See chapter 13 for a detailed explanation of the Hofstede 6D model.

If such is the case or if you're simply interested in diving a bit deeper, we invite you to measure your own cultural preference using the tool on our website (see page 38)

Your most important task at the beginning of each negotiation is to determine which of the seven mindsets your counterpart belongs to. Though their national culture's mindset is the best place to start, you cannot assume that the individual you are dealing with will behave according to the average mindset of his or her country. However, you can be quite sure that he or she does fit into one of our seven mindsets.

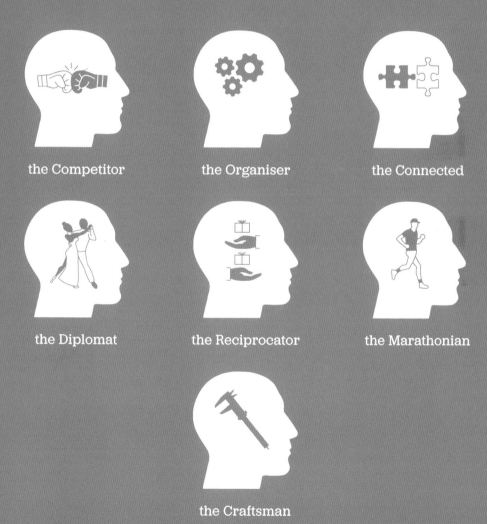

the Competitor   the Organiser   the Connected

the Diplomat   the Reciprocator   the Marathonian

the Craftsman

Measure your personal cultural preferences using Hofstede Insights' Culture Compass™

Since your own cultural programming will more than likely be different from the average of your home country, this survey will measure your personal preferences in terms of Hofstede's model. The Culture Compass™ helps you visualise the impact of your own cultural value preferences as well as potential behavioural pitfalls.

The detailed report you will receive by email will give you:
- your own scores on the 6 dimensions
- the scores of your home country
- the scores of your country of interest
- detailed personalized advice based on a comparison of your personal scores to the average value pattern of the country of your interest
- a list of countries most similar to your own preferences
- a list of countries most different from your own preferences

GET YOUR 50% DISCOUNT!

Please go to www.hofstede-insights.com/culture-compass, select the option 'as a negotiator', choose the country you're interested in and start the survey.

By entering the code: **NEGOSTYLE**, you will receive a 50 % discount on the regular price for this online tool.

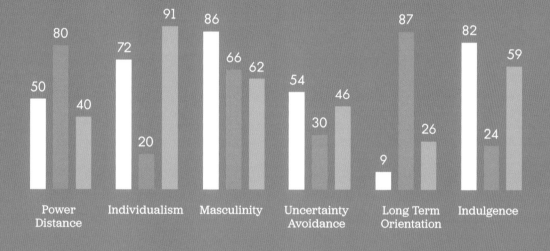

	Power Distance	Individualism	Masculinity	Uncertainty Avoidance	Long Term Orientation	Indulgence
You	50	72	86	54	9	82
China	80	20	66	30	87	24
United States	40	91	62	46	26	59

● You

● China

● United States

5.1 Negotiation is a **contest** (chapter 6)

The first MINDSET is negotiating with the 'Competitor'. This mental image may conjure up images ranging from a wrestling match, where brute force is as important as skill, to a martial arts competition, where it's all about skill and technique, to a game of chess, where everything is dependent on strategy. Any of these factors may apply, depending on the person you are negotiating with. But the core mindset of your counterpart is 'competition'. It is a confrontation with the aim being to win. It is survival of the fittest with little mercy or sympathy for the loser.

How can you detect this mindset?
Listen carefully to his priorities and to the vocabulary he uses. There is a high probability you will detect some of the following words: challenge, achievement, 'let's make it happen', short-term success, winning, quick solution, targets.

Some questions you might ask to detect this mindset:
- Why are you interested into our product?
- What would make you change supplier?
- What would convince you?
- What is stopping you working with us?
- How much time do you have to solve...?
- What is your target?

The countries with the highest propensity for this mindset are the Anglo-Saxon countries. (US, UK, Australia, New Zealand...)

5.2 Negotiation is a **process** (chapter 7)

The second MINDSET is negotiating with the 'Organiser'. You will almost certainly have encountered this type of negotiator. Careful, planned and organised, they are the champions of what we call the process mindset. Carefully respecting an agreed process for the negotiation is at least as (if not more) important than the actual objective of the negotiation. They are looking for a partner that fits at all levels and can seamlessly integrate like a well-fitting cog in their machine. Ask them what their negotiation process is, what the steps are that you need to follow, what the stages are that you need to go through and then scrupulously follow them, so that at the end of the process, closing the deal is almost a predetermined outcome.

How can you detect this mindset?
Listen carefully to his priorities and to the vocabulary he uses. There is a high probability you will detect some of the following words: expertise, structure, information, transparency, organisation, process, reliability, references, technical, predictability.

Some questions you might ask to detect this mindset:
- What is your decision process?
- Who is involved in the decision-making process?
- Can your expert in… meet our expert?
- How are your competitors doing?
- Could you share the test results you achieved with….?

The countries with the highest propensity for this mindset are the Germanic countries (Germany, Austria, Czech Republic, German speaking Switzerland...)

5.3   Negotiation is a search for win-win (chapter 8)

The third MINDSET is negotiating with the 'Connected'. There is a lot of talk about the search for a win-win solution being the holy grail of negotiation. One finds it in lots of books, at universities and in sales trainings, but the reality is that one doesn't encounter it as often as one would be led to believe. Most of us tend to be stuck in a different mindset. Nevertheless, it exists. The connected truly see a negotiation, not as a quest to win, but as a search for a win-win conclusion to the benefit of all parties. The Connected negotiator is unusually well informed, has an extended network, is very open and direct and expects the same of you. After all, you can only find a win-win solution if each party is honest and straightforward so that together you can find the best possible outcome for all involved. The successful outcome is a long-term, true partnership for the benefit of all.

How can you detect this mindset?
Listen carefully to his priorities and to the vocabulary he uses. There is a high probability you will detect some of the following words: consensus, creative solution, innovation, 'let's find a solution together', cooperative, well-being, common interest.

Some questions you might ask to detect this mindset:

· What can we do together to solve...?
· What do you really need/want?
· I cannot meet all your expectations but do you think we can find a creative solution together?
· If we start working together, how will the change of supplier be handled?

The countries with the highest propensity for this mindset are the Scandinavian countries and the Netherlands.

5.4 Negotiation is a **diplomatic ballet** (chapter 9)

The fourth MINDSET is negotiating with the 'Diplomat'. Usually well-educated and with a sense of humour, the Diplomat can appear very kind and agreeable but also quite distant. This trait is quite specific to him. Multiple visits and meetings will be needed − a first one to introduce yourself and your company, another to break the ice and start to establish a relationship, a third one to show stamina as well as respect. In short, this is a real diplomatic ballet, which involves taking little steps forward and making time to grow closer and get to know each other better. The mindset of the Diplomat negotiator revolves around the idea that one doesn't do business with just anyone and one needs to prove oneself to be regarded as an acceptable counterpart.

How can you detect this mindset?
Listen carefully to his priorities and to the vocabulary he uses. There is a high probability you will detect some of the following words: philosophy, centralised organisation, rules, reliable, formality, honour, logical, make sense, elegant solutions.

Some questions you might ask to detect this mindset:
· In principle, do you mind changing suppliers?
· What would the philosophy of our partnership be?
· It simply seems logical for our organisations to develop a partnership. Do you share that view?
· I think we found an elegant compromise. Do you agree?
· Do you agree that it makes sense for us to work together?

The countries with the highest propensity for this mindset are the Latin countries (France, Spain, Northern Italy, Belgium...)

5.5 Negotiation is an **exchange of favours** (chapter 10)

 The fifth MINDSET is negotiating with the 'Reciprocator'. We find that this type of negotiation is much more prevalent than one might think. The Reciprocator is not really looking to buy a product, but rather to buy something from someone they trust. The main issue is trust in the person one deals with. Then, once he buys from you, he considers he has done you a favour and expects a favour in return. Over time we have come to realise that the higher one moves up in a hierarchy, the more prevalent this type of negotiation becomes. It's not really the exchange of a service or a product for money but rather the mutual exchange of favours. Politics functions a lot like this almost regardless of where one is in the world.

How can you detect this mindset?
Listen carefully to his priorities and to the vocabulary he uses. There is a high probability you will detect some of the following words: trust, long-term deal, loyalty, references, introductions, implicit, respect, centralisation, uncomfortable with change, relationships are more important than successful execution of tasks.

Some questions you might ask to detect this mindset:
- During my next visit, may I invite you for lunch or dinner?
- I have a friend who would like to do an internship in your country. Do you know someone who could help her?
- Is your company a family company?
- Would you be interested in visiting our main factory (or HQ)?

The countries with the highest propensity for this mindset can be found in Eastern Europe, Africa and South America.

5.6   Negotiation is a **marathon** (chapter 11)

 The sixth MINDSET is negotiating with the 'Marathonian'. This is the negotiator who never seems to be able to make a decision, never truly closes a deal, and even if he does, he revisits whatever agreement you've made all the time because this or that circumstance has changed. Often, the conclusion of a deal, the signed contract, only signifies the beginning of the negotiation. It signifies that enough trust has been established to begin working together, but there is an expectation that you will be flexible and adaptable enough during the contract time to make whatever changes are necessary as and when circumstances change. The Western, sequential, straight line approach is alien to him.

How can you detect this mindset?
Listen carefully to his priorities and to the vocabulary he uses. There is a high probability you will detect some of the following words: references, introductions, comfortable with change, gaining face, philosophy of project, information, relationships are more important than successful execution of tasks.

Some questions you might ask to detect this mindset:
- How important is this project for your company?
- Would it be easy for you to change supplier?
- How important is it for you to have signed contract / to have clear specifications?
- May I invite you for lunch or dinner?
- Would you be interested in visiting our main factory (or HQ)?

The countries with the highest propensity of this mindset are found in Asia.

5.7 Negotiation is a **search for perfection** (chapter 12)

 The seventh and final MINDSET is negotiating with the 'Craftsman'. Focused on the relationship first, the Craftsman sees the big picture as well as each tiny detail as important. Nothing escapes the Craftsman. He will not do business with you until you have established a considerable level of trust, and will search for a harmonious deal while continuously making sure that every little aspect of the deal is perfect.

We see this mainly in Japan and have found that negotiating with anyone of this mindset is a very different experience from negotiating anywhere else in the world.

How can you detect this mindset?
Listen carefully to his priorities and to the vocabulary he uses. There is a high probability you will detect some of the following words: precision, expertise, planning, efficiency, reliability, no risk solution, good reputation, proven success, long term, continuity, resilience.

This search for perfection gives the impression that there is little sense of priority, and that this mindset considers everything as equally important. Therefore, be prepared to answer hundreds of questions about details right from the start!

Some questions you might ask to detect this mindset:
- What is your decision process and who is involved?
- What is your planning?
- What have you budgeted to realise this?
- What are your quality requirements?
- Could we have a drink later tonight?

CHAPTER 6

Mindset 1:

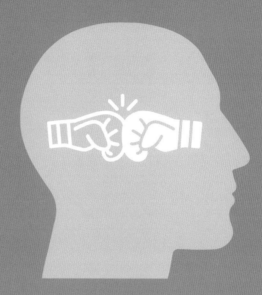

Negotiating with the 'Competitor'

6

KEY WORDS: individualistic · egalitarian · result-oriented · live to work · short-term focus · contest · competition · winning · innovation · achievement

6.1   Why do we call them the Competitors?

In our vocabulary, we characterise the Competitor as very individualistic, highly egalitarian, self-motivated, comfortable with uncertainty, always prepared for a contest or to have a fight and usually expecting short-term results.

The key to understanding this first mindset is that it's all about the individual. Globally, the US, Australia and the UK occupy the top three places on individualism index, (with scores of 91, 90 and 89 respectively), which is why you are likely to encounter this mindset in Anglo-Saxon societies. In his book[6], Hofstede speculates that it may not be a coincidence that English is the only language in which the word 'I' is always written with a capital letter.

As the UK is one of the countries that operates with the mindset of the competitor, we have chosen to set our examples there.

Here, we enter a world where things are relatively simple and straightforward… for the customer. Doing business and making a profit is 'natural'. Competition is good for society, risk taking is part of everyday life, people are proud to be ambitious and each person is responsible for themselves. Only the result counts, but failure is nothing to be afraid of because it is the cost of learning on the path to success. The best way to experience the Competitor mindset is to watch a bit of Prime Minister's Question Time on BBC parliament television. If you've never watched it before and you're not from a Competitor country, prepare to be shocked.

Once you've understood this mindset and have adapted to its values, the Competitors are relatively easy to negotiate with as everything is pretty straightforward.

For the Competitors, the game is never over until it's over. The manner in which London won the bid to host the Summer Olympics in 2012 is the perfect example of this. The contest was between Paris and London. The French team produced a beautiful, well-polished and extremely thorough proposal, confident that the superior infrastructure of Paris and their attention to detail would secure them the bid. In contrast, London's infrastructure left a lot to be desired. There were no modern stations to speak off, a heavily saturated road network and insufficient hotel capacity. In short, everything needed to be constructed. The English press was already looking

6   Cultures and Organizations, Software of the Mind

for a scape goat to blame the failure of the bid on. However, for Tony Blair's team, the fight wasn't over yet. The question was simple: how is the final decision made? The answer: by 104 votes. The conclusion: we need 53 votes!

Tony Blair, unwilling to give up the fight until it was over, decided to personally lead his already very active team of lobbyists all over the world. In the end, they succeeded… by scraping together 54 votes.

Before we get into the specifics of how to negotiate with the Competitor, there are a few principles that guide his mindset which can be invaluable to know.

6.1.1   The negotiation is a contest

If, for some cultures, negotiation is an exercise in diplomacy, or the search of win/win, or a marathon, for the Competitors, it's a contest. For them, it is exciting, allows them to constantly measure themselves and improve their self-esteem, even if sometimes they hit the deck. Losing is just a part of the game. When they lose, they take in good spirits and will probably go and have a beer with their adversary at the nearest pub.

Since we have used the analogy of sports, how about the notion of fair play? While fair play may be applied to the individual, it is largely irrelevant to the game. A commercial negotiation or commercial relationship doesn't have many rules, if any at all. (It is a matter of debate whether the methods used by Tony Blair to achieve the required votes for the Summer Olympics were 'fair'…)

It is important to understand that in a contest, you are the equal of the buyer. A contest is played between two individuals or teams that are deemed to be on the same or sufficiently similar level. The customer is important but he is NOT the king, unlike in many other cultures. 'May the best win' is the standard mindset.

6.1.2   The use of first names

As the Competitors are very egalitarian, the use of first names is very common. Except in the UK, which retains some aspects of a class-sensitive society, the use of titles is also unusual. Do not make the mistake of thinking that this shows a lack of respect.

6.1.3   'We are not the company'

When you negotiate with a Competitor, she will see you and observe you carefully, just like an athlete observes her opponent before the match. Don't be surprised if a Competitor, albeit discretely, criticises her own company or her boss. She is an individual who works for one company today and may work for its competitor tomorrow, if they will pay her more. If she critiques your company and you are from a very different cultural background, you may feel insulted or attacked. Try to understand that it is not meant as an insult.

In essence, the individual fulfils a role or a function for the company that employs her and she is financially rewarded for that. No more, no less. The relationship between the individual and the company she works for is a pure business transaction and there are no other expectations from either the company or the individual.

It is easy to see how you can use this state of mind, and this particular relationship between the individual and his or her employer, to your advantage. For instance, it is perfectly acceptable during a negotiation to say something like: "If you were in my shoes, you would refuse what you are asking me now." Your counterpart will probably reply: "You are right, but if you were in my shoes, you'd ask for the same." This perfectly illustrates the mindset of the Competitor. Let's play the game and fight as hard as we can whilst recognising each other as individuals. It is important to understand that for a competitor, nothing is ever personal – it's just business. This significantly de-dramatizes situations which would lead to a lot of stress and high emotions in other cultures.

6.1.4   Emotion is a sign of weakness

In a business setting, Competitors really dislike displays of emotion. You might even say that they hate it. For them, business is business, you need to be able to call a cat a cat without involving emotion. Beware, if she tells you that you are 'too emotional', your counterpart is actually insulting you. For a Competitor, emotion has no place in business. This is very different in many other cultures. Southern European or Latin-American may find this particularly challenging.

A PERSONAL ANECDOTE:
During one of Jean-Pierre's routine visits to a company that was in financial difficulties, the purchasing manager announced at the beginning of the meeting that they wouldn't be seeing each other anymore because his own contract was going to be terminated. Since he explained this to Jean-Pierre in a rather matter of fact way, he was intrigued and asked how he could so calmly accept this. Wasn't he disappointed? He told Jean-Pierre he'd receive a decent 'golden

handshake' and that, in any case, he understood the sums. "They don't have any other choice than to streamline the company and let me go."

For the Competitor, business is just a game of sums. Note that you can use this idea to underpin your arguments or refuse a price reduction. NEVER EVER use emotional arguments to present your case. Always remain factual, numeric and pragmatic.

6.1.5   Comfortable with uncertainty

This is a very important element in understanding the Competitor. Typically, the Competitor is not afraid and can comfortably leave a negotiation with a significant amount of uncertainty. Competitors are confident that, somehow, things will always work out in the end. This enables them to take big risks more easily, apply poker strategies and bluff their way through negotiations. In some other cultures, the ultimate fear that limits them is the fear of failure. This does not apply to the Competitor.

A PERSONAL ANECDOTE:

Early on in Jean-Pierre's career, after having been very successful in Belgium, he moved to the UK to take up a similar position. The target was to increase gross sales as well as improve profitability, just like he had done in Belgium. Because of the exceptional quality of the company's product, they were the only supplier able to provide copier paper with a 100 % functional guarantee. Jean-Pierre had managed to convince all of his Belgian customers to sell their product under the company's brand name rather than selling it under their own name. For the customers, there was the advantage of lower inventory, but they did lose some control on the marketing of the product. Some customers didn't like this but in the end, every customer accepted Jean-Pierre's strategy and started selling the product under the company's brand name.

Having arrived in the UK, Jean-Pierre started out by meeting all his distributors to try to understand their needs. He was convinced he'd be able to deploy the same strategy and consequently set out to convert one of his medium-sized distributors. The distributor was a young dynamic individual who'd set up his business quite recently and was very successful. Jean-Pierre admits that he expected him to be 'easy prey' because he'd noticed that the man's success was based on the exceptional quality of his product, which represented 75 % of his sales.

When Jean-Pierre explained to him that he could no longer supply the product under the distributor's brand but that, on the other hand, the distributor would make significant savings due to reduction of inventory, the distributor replied that there was no way he could accept Jean-Pierre's proposal. He completely agreed that it was the exceptional product quality which had allowed him to quickly build up his business but stated clearly that he had no intention of abandoning selling the product under his own brand name.

After the distributor paid the restaurant bill, they each went their own way. As they do in Belgium, Jean-Pierre said they'd meet again to re-discuss after some period of reflection.

With a big smile, the distributor said that Jean-Pierre could try as long as he'd like but that he'd never give up his brand. Despite these words, Jean-Pierre wasn't in the least worried and remained confident that they would be able to come to a deal. How wrong he was.

A mere two hours later, the distributor sent Jean-Pierre a fax in which he cancelled all current orders and ended their relationship. He added the following PS: 'I clearly understood you're hell-bent on selling exclusively under your own brand. So let's not waste each other's time!'

In Belgium, which is Jean-Pierre's 'normal', they would have taken the time to discuss, to negotiate, to find a compromise. The courageous Brit, fixed on his objective to build his brand, didn't hesitate to walk away from their relationship simply because Jean-Pierre's commercial strategy was no longer compatible with his own objectives. The fact that Jean-Pierre's proposal would have improved his finances was completely irrelevant for him.

Jean-Pierre's problem was cultural. He had applied his own cultural framework, his own 'normal', to an environment that is substantially different. The Belgian culture, as well as the French, has a need for certainty. They feel uncomfortable when situations are not clear and will strive to minimise uncertainty. They have very high scores on the uncertainty avoidance dimension. (Belgium: 94, France: 86)

Unfortunately for Jean-Pierre, the British culture is opposite in this *regard. Brits are very comfortable with uncertainty and are confident that things will work out in the end. Unconsciously, Jean-Pierre's commercial approach was based on his customer's need to minimise uncertainty. The UK's score for uncertainty avoidance is 35. It took Jean-Pierre quite some time to realise this but ultimately, he managed to adapt and fine-tune his commercial approach to the British cultural framework.*

6.1.6   Short term orientation

Life, for the competitor, is a series of contests, so short-term wins are important. Rare are the companies that have a five- or ten-year plan. The focus on the results of the current quarter almost always outweigh the importance of a longer term strategic view. Just compare the energy policy of Germany with the energy policies of the UK and the US. Germany takes the long-term view and is phasing out fossil and nuclear sources to replace them with renewables. The UK just approved a new investment in nuclear energy which has benefits today but shifts the environmental burden to the future. The US continues to focus on fossil fuel because of the availability of shale gas and oil, choosing for cheap energy today and leaving the impact of climate change as a burden for the future.

6.1.7   British politeness

During a training session in a multinational company, someone made the following remark: "The Brits are known for their politeness. Isn't that a contradiction with the concept of a contest"?

The answer is that it is important to understand that culture develops over a long time and allows people to live together in a society. It is exactly because the Brits are Competitors (individualist, invested in success and proud), that creates the need for rules regarding behaviour. Imagine what might have happened if they hadn't invented the idea of queuing at the bus stop…!

One other thing that is very specific to the British culture is the use of understatements and implied messages. Brits are masters at disguising their true message, and unless you've grown up in the UK, you'll probably find this hard to decipher and may find yourself regularly wrong-footed. The British really enjoy using this to irritate Americans and Australians. Even other native English speakers struggle to understand what the British are really saying, so just imagine how difficult it is for non-native English speakers. The following selection from the famous table "What the Brits say and what they really mean…"[7] is good illustration:

---

[7]   The author of this widely published table is unknown.

WHAT THEY SAY	WHAT THEY MEAN	WHAT IS UNDERSTOOD
I hear what you say	I disagree and do not wish to discuss this any further	He accepts my point of view
With the greatest respect	I think you are wrong (or a fool)	He is listening to me
Not bad	Good or very good	Poor or mediocre
Perhaps you would like to think about / I would suggest/ It would be nice if	This is an order. Do it or be prepared to bear the consequences.	Think about the idea but do what you like
Oh by the way / Incidentally	This is the primary purpose of our conversation	This is not very important
I was a bit disappointed / It is a pity that you	I am most upset and cross	It does not really matter
Very interesting	I don't agree / I don't believe you	They are impressed
Could we consider some other options?	I don't like your idea	They have not yet decided
I'll bear it in mind	I will do nothing about it	They will probably do it
Please think about that some more	It's a bad idea. Don't do it	Good idea, keep developing it
I am sure it is my fault	It is your fault!	It was their fault
That is an original point of view	You must be crazy	They like my ideas
You must come for dinner...sometime	Not an invitation, just being polite	I will get an invitation soon
Quite good	A bit disappointing	Quite good

RECAP:

· Business is strictly separate from personal relationships
· A job is just a job, there is very little emotional attachment to the company
· Use of first names
· Short-term focus
· Business first, control your emotions
· Replace the fear of losing with an eagerness to win
· Be a good sport: do your best all the time, come what may

LIST OF COMPETITOR COUNTRIES	Australia, Canada, Ireland, New Zealand South Africa (white), UK, USA

This cluster of countries is typified as having Competitor societies. In the table below, we have listed the scores of the US and the UK in the Hofstede 6D model as they are representative of the group of countries. You can use the last column for your home country's or your own score.

	USA	UK	TYPICAL CHARACTERISTICS FOR THE CLUSTER	YOUR SCORE[8]
Power distance	40	35	Low	
Individualism	91	89	High	
Masculinity	62	66	High	
Uncertainty avoidance	46	35	Low to medium	
Long Term Orientation	26	51	Low to medium	
Indulgence vs Restraint	68	69	High	

8 Please see page 38 on how to determine your own score.

6.2　The 6 steps of the sales process with the Competitor

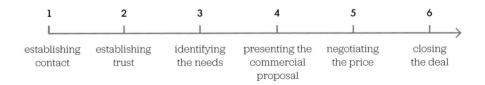

1	2	3	4	5	6
establishing contact	establishing trust	identifying the needs	presenting the commercial proposal	negotiating the price	closing the deal

6.2.1　Establishing contact

Generally speaking, customer prospection is pretty straightforward. The egalitarian aspect of Competitor societies (low power distance scores) assures the supplier is respected as a person regardless of whether the products or services are required or not. You are a sales person, and your job is just as respectable as any other. First names are used straight away.

Again, one peculiarity of the UK is that you may be surprised by how much time and attention the buyer gives you. But then you may be surprised again, when you try to contact them afterwards, to find out that they are not actually interested in your products or services at all. British politeness has no boundaries. We can't tell you how many times that, judging by the reaction of the buyer, both of us have been optimistic following a first meeting without understanding that it really reflected British politeness rather than a genuine interest in our products. Be aware of the potential loss of time. A Brit may like you, invite you to the pub for a drink and have no interest in your products whatsoever. He's simply interested in you as a person.

To arrange a meeting, a simple phone call, preferably on his mobile is enough. You'll be evaluated on the first couple of sentences you use. They must be clear, concise, to the point and attract his attention to the advantages you have to offer. They call this the 'elevator pitch'. Imagine you're in an elevator with Marc Zuckerberg, the inventor of Facebook. You have one minute face-to-face with him. What are you going to tell him so that he is interested enough to give you meeting? This pitch needs to be really carefully prepared.

A meeting is relatively simple to obtain. It is obviously easier if your company is well known in the sector. However, Competitors are more than willing to give start-ups an opportunity because they are obsessed with 'not missing an opportunity'. If this is the situation you find yourself in, make sure you say something like "The market doesn't know us yet but it won't be long", or "You have priority over your competitors" during your elevator pitch.

You are probably familiar with the typology of the 'hunter-salesman' versus the 'farmer-salesman'. The first is very good at recruiting new customers but finds it more difficult to nurture an enduring relationship with them. The second has the opposite characteristics. Not surprisingly, this concept was developed in the USA where it is wholly fitting. Many European companies successfully apply the concept as well. Whichever type of salesman you are naturally, in your dealings with the Competitors, be a hunter. More specifically, be a relaxed, fun-loving hunter who puts people at ease very early on in the relationship. Competitors really appreciate this.

Depending on your own cultural framework or profile, this may be very hard and represent a real culture shock. You may see it as normal, or even more respectful, to be a bit reserved in the presence of the customer. For Competitors, such an attitude can result in a massive misunderstanding. You may be considered disingenuous or snobby, as that's the attitude the British upper classes sometimes adopt.

6.2.2   Establishing trust

Well done, you've managed to get a meeting. Be aware that the Competitors are egalitarian and the idea that 'the customer is king' doesn't really apply as much as in some other cultures. Avoid being too polite or too formal. A little bit of small talk before getting to the meat of the subject is the way to get to know each other, and provides an opportunity for both sides to 'judge' their opponent. If you struggle with small talk, simply say something self-deprecating and they'll appreciate it a lot. For Brits, self-deprecation is the ultimate form of humour.

Depending on the sector of activity and/or the product or service you are trying to sell, the game will be different. If you're selling a machine or a service, it will be a simple and direct game. If the sector is a part of a chain, such as distribution, IT or finance, the game is more like the establishment of a partnership to fight the market. The ultimate goal is not just the price but rather the market share you and the customer will be able to obtain together. You need to figure out, depending on your sector, how to consider your customer. Is she an adversary you need to conquer or is she a future partner?

The way to establish trust with the Competitor is to be transparent, clear and coherent in your communication and behaviour. She's interested in finding out how you work, or 'how you tick'. It doesn't matter at all if your way is totally different from hers. She's not afraid of that. She doesn't need you to be on her side. What does matter to her is that she understands how you tick so she can anticipate your behaviour. If you're a tennis or golf player, it is perfectly acceptable to invite the Competitor for a game, to break the ice. For her, it's another opportunity to find out how you tick and the same goes for you.

Remember, countries in the Competitor cluster have a high score on individualism dimension. What drives the Competitor is finding out how you can help him personally. To motivate the individualist, simply make it clear to him how you can help him be more successful. Let us be absolutely clear that we are not talking about some kind of extra-legal benefit for him personally, but we are suggesting you show him exactly how you can make him more successful by making his organisation more successful. Sales arguments like "If you adopt our formula, thanks to you, your company will profit…" are wholly appropriate ways of presenting one's value proposition to the Competitor.

A word on conversation etiquette. In most of the Southern countries, it is perfectly acceptable to interrupt each other during a conversation. It's a way of signalling that you're paying attention, that you understand each other. In a conversation with a Competitor this is inappropriate. One waits until the other has finished his argument or sentence. A pause in the conversation, a bit of reflection or even a little hesitation is perfectly acceptable. The Competitor will not think you're an illiterate idiot, we promise. Also, if you're not a native English speaker, don't worry about your foreign accent. Mostly it is perceived as cute. The Competitors, (even the British), do not consider themselves as the owners of their language. Your English, as long as it's understandable is as acceptable as theirs. They'll never mock you for butchering the pronunciation of their language, contrary to what happens in many other countries.

6.2.3 Identifying the needs

What are we talking about here? Obviously, we list the needs of the customer and align our proposal with those. Following the analogy, we've chosen for the Competitor, you need to identify the rules of the game. Which products are appropriate? Who are the players? What is the market price level (so you know where you need to be to be able to conclude the deal)? Who is the competition? This will allow you to develop a common base with your counterpart and begin the game. All this will depend on your sector of activity. Will it be a competition between two opponents or will you try to form a partnership? It is up to you to analyse the situation and decide.

STRAIGHT-TALKING:
You will have understood by now that it's all about clarity, precision and solution-oriented communication. Avoid phrases like 'I'll see what I can do for you' when you know very well that you have no room for manoeuvre and no solution to offer. If you say this, Competitors will just see this as an irritating loss of time. You're far better off making it clear that there's nothing else you can do, or that you can't do it for this or that reason. You might offer alternative and better solutions but be careful not to be perceived as 'lecturing'. This happened to Jean-Pierre once, as he'd forgotten that the

Brits, just like all other countries in our group, score high on the masculinity dimension. You might be perceived as arrogant if you try to sell them an alternative solution, as they may see it as you telling them what to do.

Establishing the needs also involves settling on a style of communication and deciding if there is potential for future partnership. Conveying your arguments in a frank manner, without emotion, is the objective. Use humour where you can, as it helps to develop a rapport that is comfortable as well as open and direct.

6.2.4   Presenting the commercial proposal

Be aware that the Competitor has a very explicit inductive approach to problem solving. They invented the concepts of 'case-based learning' and 'best practices'. Make sure you don't bore them to death with a deductive approach, which would rely heavily on explaining background theory. The Competitor simply won't find this interesting or relevant.

This is YOUR moment and YOUR show. The Competitors admire that you're a salesman. The presentation and the impression you make are highly important. Use all the means you have at your disposal to seduce and convince your counterpart. That is what's expected of you. Use whatever tools you have – seduction, humour, a description of benefits for your customer (financial or otherwise). Your customer expects to play a good match and to enjoy the battle.

The tools to develop presentations were invented by the Competitors. A PowerPoint presentation is today's classic tool but you can be as imaginative as you like and use any tool you have at your disposal. Remember that the Competitor wants a good show, so the more effort you put in using demos, videos, on-site tests, role-play, etc. the more the presentation will be appreciated, as long as it remains pragmatic and solution-oriented. In some cultures, it is considered inelegant to be too much of a salesman and sales people tend to under-sell. Not so for the Competitors. Selling is your job so you are expected to be the best you can be. It is very important that you display self-confidence to inspire confidence in your product.

This is most extreme in the USA where over-selling tends to be the norm. Because she is used to over-selling, your counterpart will automatically take everything you say with a grain of salt and downplay your statements and claims in her own mind. Imagine, now, that you are under-selling, or even level-selling (using only statements and arguments that are 100% accurate), as you might normally do, but imagine that you are competing with an American company for the same piece of business. Since your customer is expecting you to over-sell your product or service, even though it might be superior, it is likely to appear inferior to whatever is offered by your American competitor. You are very unlikely to get the business unless you play the game the American way.

6

WHICH ARE THE ARGUMENTS THAT MAKE A DIFFERENCE?

If you look at Geert Hofstede's country scores for the Competitors, you'll find excellent guidance. You'll want to spend sufficient time and effort preparing and adjusting your arguments, and making sure you are presenting them in the order of importance they have for your counterpart.

Competitors like:
· Performance
· Reputation and status
· Personal advancement
· Ambition

Let's use our example of the wristwatch with a new concept that we're trying to sell to a local dealer. You need to focus on the fact that this new development has fantastic performance (e.g. precision of timekeeping), that in buying one, the owner will belong to a small exclusive group of owners (e.g. Bill Gates also ordered one), that there will be considerable profit generated for the dealer by selling this watch and that he'll have exclusive distribution of this watch in the region.

THE PROPOSAL

You will already have discussed the price at length during the previous phase and there won't be any suspense with regards to that. A formal document is not necessary. If a PowerPoint presentation holds all of the elements, a PDF copy of that is more than sufficient. Alternatively, a simple email with all the details is enough. Depending on your own company's cultural framework, your internal requirements for formal documentation may be a lot stricter than your customer's.

It is really important to keep it simple. If at all possible, present an all-in price. If you have the opportunity, go to a car dealership and just observe the way they sell cars. As we've said, you'll find a large sign on top of the car with a single price on it. Which options does the car have? Most likely it is 'full option', and has all of them. The masculine side of the Competitor only wants the best. You will rarely see a pricing scheme for a car starting from a base price and then adding a whole list of options, so don't do it for your proposal either.

6.2.5   Negotiating the price

Because the price is absolutely vital for the Competitor, you will have discussed this in much detail when identifying the needs (step 3).

Now your negotiation skills are being called upon. You need to feel where the boundary is, and sense how far you can go. Generally, Competitors are good sports.

6

They can live with the fact that you'll try to strong-arm them but they need to score points as well. Make sure you integrate that into your strategy.

Also, don't forget that the Competitors, and particularly the British, can be very charming. A bit of relaxation time, such as a game of golf or tennis, or a beer at the local pub, can be part of the negotiation process. For some of you, this may be difficult to explain to your own organisation. While the whole process is a like a game, you will find that there is a real humane side as well, because the Competitor respects his or her counterpart for who they are as an individual.

6.2.6   Closing the deal

What happens when your proposal is better than your competition's or the existing supplier's?

You'll have the deal, no doubt about it. As we will see later on, buyers in other cultures can be embarrassed when confronted with this reality because they have to discard an existing supplier in order to give the business to you. This means upsetting or ending a relationship. Not so for the Competitors. You have won, which means you take the place, because THE WINNER TAKES IT ALL!

You may be surprised by the formal nature the closing of the deal can take. Generally, you'll have an animated discussion during which each side defends their turf vigorously. At one point, usually after you've made a concession, there will be a silence. Your counterpart will stand up, shake your hand and say "we have a deal".

Once you have obtained this 'handshake deal', typically, formal documentation will need to follow describing every aspect of the deal in minute detail, but nothing will change anymore. The handshake is the deal. This is very different from many other cultures where this would only be a first step, and really not much more than a declaration of intent, while many aspects still need to be negotiated and may change with time and circumstance.

Not so with the Competitors. The deal is the deal and nothing will change that. This is one of the reasons why contracts with Competitors can be so elaborate. They try to anticipate every possible 'what if' scenario, so that the contract can be respected no matter what. It is important to understand that the contract **IS** the relationship – nothing more, nothing less. Most markedly in the US, the more detailed and elaborate the contract is, the more comfortable the Competitor feels and the more trusting the relationship will be. Again, this is very different from many other cultures where the human relationship and personal trust come first and the contract is secondary and flexible.

It is comforting to know that once you've won the deal it **IS** the deal and it's absolutely final. However, know that now you are the incumbent supplier, what happened to the previous supplier may well happen to you. One day, you may find yourself out of the door again without even the smallest warning sign.

6

- · Prepare your elevator pitch
- · Be positive and insistent
- · Behave as if you're visiting common friends
- · Be yourself
- · Be as clear and transparent as you can be
- · Be prepared to capture the correct meaning of what the British say
- · Make sure you understand and answer the personal needs of your counterpart

NEGOTIATING WITH THE COMPETITORS

1	Establishing contact	A simple phone call may be enough. Prepare your elevator pitch. Avoid impersonal emails. Use a reference whenever you can.
2	Establishing trust	A bit of small talk, especially with a foreigner, before tackling the business at hand. Beware of 'What the Brits say...', use humour and be relaxed. It's the moment before the start of the game when the opponents are judging each-other.
3	Identifying the needs	Establish the basis for the relationship with clarity and simplicity. She's looking for X, you can offer Y and you'd like to convince her that maybe Y is the best solution. You listen to her needs and then discuss openly and honestly what you can and cannot do for her. Let her know if you're not clear on something and/or need to discuss it internally. Don't hesitate to communicate your own cultural background and use it jokingly and humbly to diffuse potential misunderstandings.
4	Presenting the commercial proposal	This is YOUR moment, YOUR show. You will be admired for the sales person you are. The quality of the show and the impression you make are important. You must go all out, use everything you have at your disposal – seduction, humour, profit. Arguments: performance, reputation, personal advancement, courage and price.

5	Negotiating the price	Count on the individualism of the buyer. What's in it for him? Don't hesitate to use phrases like *'thanks to you, your company will… and you will…'*. The price is the score of the match. You will probably conclude the deal with a handshake which is a powerful symbol that the deal is done.
6	Closing the deal	What happens when you are competitive? The deal will be done quickly. Before you leave, you'll know when you'll get the order. The incumbent supplier is OUT.

Mindset 2:

Negotiating with the 'Organiser'

7

KEY WORDS: egalitarian · principals · structure · organisation · system · expertise · process · clockwork · reliability · quality

7.1   Why do we call them the Organisers?

They appreciate order, punctuality and precision, seem hierarchical and don't mind obeying orders. However, contrary to some very hierarchical cultures, they do not obey orders just because they come from a boss, but rather because they understand that coordination and coherence are important and they believe that the boss is more capable than themselves. He is an expert in the field, has an overview of everything and is therefore best qualified to be the leader.

In our vocabulary, we characterise this person as very individualistic, not impressed by hierarchy, quite self-motivated, having a major problem with uncertainty and focused on the mid to long term. As Germany is a typical Organiser country, we chose it as the basis for this chapter.

Before we dive into the specifics of how to negotiate with the Organisers, there are several principles that guide their mindset that you need to familiarise yourself with.

7.1.1   The Organiser is very process-minded

The Organiser's mindset functions in a very deductive way and thus there is a very strong need to understand why something works, is better or is cheaper.

You may find it hard to deal with, but the concept of process, or the right way to do things step-by step, is omnipresent in their society. There's a need for a framework to do things in – for certainty, control, rituals and procedures. You will find that for every change Organisers have procedures which outline how to make the change, meaning there are procedures to change procedures…

There's no point in trying to resist it; you simply need to know, understand and adapt to this reality. Try and be the first to offer a solution to a problem and your solution will become the reference point. Most likely, you'll be the supplier for a long time to come.

We'll come back to this later but we recommend you ask your counterpart about his organisation, about their decision-making process and who the decision makers are. It is especially important to find out if there are any experts involved, as they may well be the hidden decision makers. Your negotiating counterpart will most likely appreciate your effort to try and understand her company but even more importantly, it'll help you enormously with your sales efforts and avoid you losing time or misunderstanding. You might even suggest some small tweaks to one process or another, and it might easily be accepted. This is one of the peculiar aspects of negotiating with the Organisers. You need to start by negotiating the actual process, deciding on what form the path to success would take, because this is really important for them. Once the process is agreed, you will be expected to follow it, step by step, in what you may consider to be excruciating detail. So be prepared to pay a lot of attention to this. The better you negotiate the process and the stricter you then follow it, the more trust you will build.

7.1.2   The perception of the organisation

When you ask an Organiser to choose an image which best represents his organisation, he will usually describe a set of interacting cogwheels. Each employee, each member of the organisation, sees himself as an individual cogwheel and perfectly understands what he needs to do to fit in and work well with the other cogwheels in the organisation. He also has a reasonable overview of the whole organisation so understands what the various cogwheels are supposed to do to make the system work. This concept is very important as it will guide most of the Organiser's behaviour and actions.

7.1.3   Functional hierarchy

The use of titles such as Mr or Mrs, or qualifications such as Dr. or Prof., is ingrained in every day interactions. Many non-Organisers are convinced that that the Organiser mindset is very hierarchical because of this formalism. It is easy to understand why one would see it like that, but the use of titles is really just a recognition of expertise and respect, rather than of hierarchy. Organisers tend to operate with a functional hierarchy, whereby the person in charge is in their position because he or she is the expert, by qualification or experience. He or she will be respected because of their expertise, not because of their position.

7.1.4   Avoidance of uncertainty

The Organiser is very open and transparent in his analysis of the problem to be solved and the pros and cons of each of the possible solutions to it. Your solution will be analysed and discussed in all openness and you're expected to play an active role

7

in this discussion. You will gain a lot of brownie points if you can actively engage with the customer in the analysis and discussion of the characteristics, advantages and disadvantages of each option. Above all, this is an impartial technical discussion and emotion or passion have no place here. This may be quite challenging for those of you with, say, a Latin background, who may feel especially uncomfortable talking about the weaker points of your own proposition. Strange as it may seem, talking openly also about the weaker aspects of your proposition compared to the competition's will actually help you gain status. The Organiser values expertise above almost anything else, so the more objective and the more knowledgeable you come across, the more he'll trust your advice, rely on you and want to conclude the negotiation successfully.

7.1.5   Be the best

Second best is never good enough for the Organiser. If you're the best in your game, and have the best technology, or the most efficient process, you have a good card to play. Organisers have an undeniable drive for excellence and consequently have very little patience for mediocracy. Many companies in Organiser societies are world-leading in their field.

7.1.6   Invest today for a better tomorrow

The Organiser generally has a long-term view. Short-term performance is important but he will not hesitate to invest today to ensure future performance and longevity of his organisation.

> A PERSONAL ANECDOTE:
> When Marc was working in the packaging industry, his German customers were always the first to make significant investments in new technology to reduce packaging weight and energy consumption, as well as to improve line efficiency. Their principle aim was to have the lowest possible TCO (Total Cost of Ownership) in the long run, and they were willing to make significant capital expenditures to achieve this. This approach was significantly different from the approach of most other customers, for whom limiting capital expenditure today was always more important than having the lowest TCO in the long run. This German drive for the lowest TCO has resulted in state-of-the-art technology development, quickly pushing many German companies into world-leading positions.

RECAP:

· Everything is about structure and process
· Transparency is important
· Titles are a recognition of expertise not hierarchy
· Reliability is important
· Excellence is a virtue, good-enough is not acceptable
· Take the long-term view

LIST OF ORGANISER COUNTRIES	Austria, Czech Republic, Germany, Hungary, Israel, Luxembourg and Switzerland (German)

This cluster of countries is typified as Organiser societies. In the table below, we have listed the scores of the Germany and Luxembourg in the Hofstede 6D model, as they are representative of this group of countries. You can add your own score or your home country's score in the last column.

	GER- MANY	LUXEM- BOURG	TYPICAL CHARACTERISTICS FOR THE CLUSTER	YOUR SCORE[9]
Power distance	35	40	Low	
Individualism	67	60	High	
Masculinity	66	50	Medium to high	
Uncertainty avoidance	65	70	High	
Long Term Orientation	83	64	High	
Indulgence vs Restraint	40	56	Low to medium	

9 Please see page 38 on how to determine your own score.

7

7.2 The 6 steps of the sales process with the Organisers

7.2.1 Establishing contact

You may be pleasantly surprised because establishing contact with an Organiser is relatively easy. The difference, from what you may be used to, is the way to do it. We recommend sending an email with a short introduction, announcing your intention to call in the next couple of days, or, even better, asking when might be a good time to call. This is already starting to look like a process, isn't it? You can also easily ask a satisfied customer to introduce you to his colleagues. You'd be astonished to see how much and how openly competitors talk to each other and recommend their suppliers to one another. In this culture, there are lots and lots of professional associations, for buyers, for dentists, for brew masters – any professional association you can think of probably exists. In most fields of business, these can be very important vectors for business development. Especially if you are a leader and expert in your field, targeting associations and establishing yourself and your company as experts can be very fruitful indeed.

7.2.2 Establishing trust

Organisers value formality quite a bit. Be sure to dress quite traditionally, especially for your first meetings. Functional status is very important in the Organiser society so pay attention to status symbols like cars. Don't be surprised to see your potential customer staring out of the window to check which kind of car you drive. Whereas in France, for instance, as a salesman, it is appropriate to arrive in a small car regardless of your position in the hierarchy of your company, in Germany we would advise even junior sales people to drive a mid-size, German build. Anyone arriving in a tiny car is usually considered too junior. If you are a senior manager, it is totally appropriate and even advisable to arrive in a high-end car, again preferably of German build.

Respect for timing is of prime importance to the Organiser. If you have an appointment at 2 pm, be sure to be at the company's door at 1:45 pm so you have time for whatever registration needs to happen and to be escorted to the meeting room. The meeting will start at exactly 2 pm. If, for whatever reason, you're going to be late, even by 5 minutes, call ahead to inform your counterpart. Being even slightly late is considered extremely impolite as they will see it as you wasting their precious time and the meeting will start off with a negative atmosphere.

Once you're in the meeting, be very formal. Address your counterpart by his formal titles and last name only. If his business card says Dr. Dr. Müller, this is not a mistake and simply means that he obtained two PhDs. You are expected to address him as Dr. Dr. Müller. It is a good idea to use someone's title several times during the conversation as it signifies respect for and recognition of your counterpart.

It is not very common to address people by their first names even after decades of a business relationship. You will notice that even amongst colleagues that work together all the time, people address each other by their formal title and last name only. This also demonstrates the barrier between professional life and private life. For Organisers, these are two completely separate worlds and a business setting is no place to talk about private life. It is considered wholly inappropriate to enquire about personal details, or to make small talk to break the ice. What does matter are business-relevant topics such as how long you've been in the industry, or what your qualifications are.

Present your company in a formal and professional manner. A professional PowerPoint presentation, personalised with the customer's logo, will do very well. Insert something related to their company so you show you are prepared and knowledgeable about their business. It will be taken as a sign of respect and will help to build trust.

7.2.3 Identifying the needs

You will realise very quickly that the customer knows what he wants and what he doesn't want. Regardless of whether you're bringing something new to the market or whether you're trying to take a competitor's business, be mindful of the importance of procedure and process. Now is the time to start talking about those things. Ask questions like:

- How will you make your choice?
- What are the criteria?
- Who will be involved in the decision-making process?
- What will be the reaction of your current supplier?
- What will be the reaction of different departments (sales, logistics, production) when asked to switch to a new supplier?
- What is the expected timing for the process?

This is where you will lay the foundations for your success or failure, where you negotiate what will determine success or failure. The outcome of this will be a set of pre-determined criteria, which, if you meet them, will assure that the business will be awarded to you. Ideally, it will look something like this: "If we can supply a product with performance XYZ, which will be approved by your Quality Assurance department as well as your Production Manager, and if the final market tests show an approval rate higher than 7 out of 10, you agree to buy X many units per year of our product at price Y starting 1st January next year."

If this feels alien and unrealistic to you, we invite you to try it out and you will find that you counterpart will happily work with you in this manner. Execute this step diligently and you're most likely to be successful.

Finally, don't forget to openly discuss your counterpart's needs, as well as the characteristics (strengths **and** weaknesses) of your solution. He'll be equally open and discuss the strengths and weaknesses of your competitor's products with you, which will allow you to better understand your customer's needs and improve your understanding of the market.

7.2.4   Presenting the commercial proposal

By now, you'll see that if you've clearly defined everything during the previous step, you will only need to follow the programme and the process you have agreed. Once you've become used to this way of working, you'll start to understand how useful and efficient this can be.

WHICH ARE THE ARGUMENTS THAT MAKE THE DIFFERENCE?
Again, Hofstede's country scores will guide us in our choice of arguments. You'll want to spend sufficient time and effort preparing and adjusting your arguments and making sure you present them in the order of importance they have for your counterpart. Organisers like:
- Expertise
- Reliability
- Clarity and predictability
- Status

So, using our example of the watch, you will need to rely on arguments such as the exports that designed and manufactured it, (possibly throw in a visit to the manufacturing plant), the extraordinary precision of timekeeping, the lifelong warranty and the status it will bring to its wearer because it is a limited edition and Bill Gates ordered one as well.

THE PROPOSAL
There's no doubt about how the Organiser wants the price to be presented. The previous step will have guided you and typically you will present a base price supplemented with what may be a long list of separately priced options and rebates

all carefully spelled out in a neat little document. Using our example of how the price of a car is typically presented in a showroom, you will find a base price for the most basic version of the car supplemented with a very long list of options which can even double the final price of the car.

7.2.5   Negotiating the price

A PERSONAL ANECDOTE:

Jean-Pierre was contacted by an important distributor seeking to replace his current supplier because of issues with irregular supply. He was asked to come for a meeting during which the distributor tells Jean-Pierre what his annual needs are and what the price level he needs to be at is. They agree on the process to be followed: sampling, comparative testing and on-site tests with customers. Simple!

Jean-Pierre returns home feeling very optimistic as he was convinced he could meet all these criteria fairly easily. He remembers thinking that this was going to be a nice deal.

Jean-Pierre followed the agreed process meticulously but as is normal in his culture, delayed the fatal moment of presentation of his price, which was obviously and deliberately higher than the requested price. Technically, everything went very well and during the next meeting, he presented his price which was 12% above the requested price. Jean-Pierre felt he defended his price very well explaining raw material costs, manufacturing costs etc., painting a picture explaining why he couldn't possibly meet the requested price. The buyer remained totally inflexible and after three more rounds, Jean-Pierre finally acquiesced to the price he wanted assuming that now the deal was done. How wrong he was!

The buyer then said he couldn't possibly start working with Jean-Pierre's company because he couldn't trust them. Jean-Pierre was taken aback by this statement and asked him to elucidate. "Well," he said, "you explained that your cost structure doesn't allow you to meet the price I need and I believe you. Regardless of this problem, you have dropped your price below your cost simply to seal the deal.

7

Soon, this will become untenable for you and you'll ask me for a price increase. I simply cannot take the risk of doing business with you knowing that you are not covering your costs." Jean-Pierre never got the business and he is convinced that his cultural illiteracy was at the heart of the problem.

What could he have done better? Rather than continuing to defend his price based on cost structure and then subsequently lowering it as a 'commercial gesture' until they both found 'the right price' as is normal in his culture, he is sure he would have been able to close the deal had he gone back to the customer explaining that given the importance of the deal, his company had reviewed their internal processes to reduce cost and were thus able to support the price level he needed. This would have reinforced the trust rather than damaged it.

7.2.6   Closing the deal

If the entire process has been followed as originally agreed, you will receive the orders without further ado. Contracts can be as simple as a one-page document recapping the essential price and performance agreements. What will happen to the supplier you're replacing? As part of the process, this problem will have been dealt with in advance. We have encountered situations where the buyer was hesitant to end the relationship with the incumbent (and strategic) supplier, but generally, this aspect will have been dealt with as part of the process. If you think it might be an issue, you can always ensure it is being dealt with early on by explicitly integrating it into the process. Your counterpart will even appreciate you bringing it up as it shows attention to detail and due care for the process.

RECAP:

- Negotiate and agree on the process that will govern your relationship
- Analyse strengths and weaknesses openly
- Eliminate uncertainty as much as possible
- Be transparent
- Simply follow the pre-agreed process and make sure NOT to deviate from it
- If you're not one yourself, make use of experts

NEGOTIATING WITH THE ORGANISERS

1	Establishing contact	A simple phone call may be enough. A title, good qualifications and/or reputation will definitely help.
2	Establishing trust	Very little or no small talk at all. You are expected to tackle the business at hand straight away. Make sure you convey the fact that you and/or your company are experts and have a strong track record of reliability.
3	Identifying the needs	First establish what their process is that you need to follow. If needed, first negotiate the process to make sure you will be able to follow it scrupulously. Ask a lot of questions to make sure you understand their buying process as well as their needs clearly. Then follow the agreed process down to the last detail.
4	Presenting the commercial proposal	This is just a formality if step 2 and 3 have been executed properly. Use arguments that accentuate performance, reliability and expertise.
5	Negotiating the price	The price is the result of a calculation. Choose your target price carefully.
6	Closing the deal	If you need to renegotiate the price, you need to renegotiate the process. Don't change the price without changing something in the cost structure (e.g. quality, service, manufacturing process).

CHAPTER 8

Mindset 3:

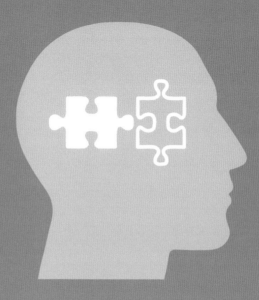

Negotiating with the 'Connected'

8

KEY WORDS: consensus · quality of life · egalitarian · work to live · social fairness · innovation · network · direct communication · win-win solutions

8.1 Why do we call them the Connected?

We characterise people in this group as individualistic, not impressed by hierarchy, very egalitarian, very connected with their peers, eager to establish consensus, quite comfortable with uncertainty and fairly long term oriented. They have sympathy for the underdog and tend to be suspicious of 'winners'. In general, quality of life is very important for them and thus some of the values that drive them are quite the opposite to those of the Competitors. They build highly connected networks of people and are constantly looking for consensus.

Before we enter further into specifics about negotiating with the Connected, here are several principles that guide their mindset.

8.1.1 The quest for balance and consensus

The Connected will strive towards the formation of partnerships that must result in a win-win situation for all. If you come from a society where competition is the norm, and winning (or defeating your counterpart) is the only thing that counts, this must be a very strange concept. However, the true goal of the Connected is to have partners rather than suppliers. Provided they are confident you are willing and able to behave in the same manner and fashion, they will remain loyal to their partners, even in difficult times.

It is important not to confuse the concept of consensus and win-win with the concept of compromise.

A compromise is typically an expedient and mutually acceptable solution which partially satisfies both parties. There are no winners or losers but it typically breeds dissatisfaction for all parties involved. Generally, it is acceptable as a short-term solution.

The quest for consensus and win-win, requires that both parties work with each other to find a solution which best satisfies the needs and concerns of each party. Because this process takes more time and effort, we talk about BUILDING a consensus versus AGREEING on a compromise. Consensus is therefore a much better base for long-term relationships than compromise is.

8.1.2   The perception of the organisation

When you ask the Connected to choose an image that best represents their society, many of them will come up with something that represents a network of well interconnected individuals. There's no particular hierarchy, everyone is everyone else's equal and there is no particular structure to the connections.

8.1.3   The market price

In no other cluster does one talk so much about the 'market price' as with the Connected. The need for consensus is expressed by a market price which is uniformly accepted as such by all the customers (the market). The market price is generally clearly established and well known by everyone. In each market, the different segments are clearly established, and because everyone plays the game the same way, your product must also fit in one of the 'boxes'. Each significant supplier will have her distribution channel. Each distributor will follow the same market segmentation so the market price will be clear. It might sound like we're starting to talk about cartels here, but we assure you that it is nothing like that.

The good side of this is that once a niche is yours, your partner will be by your side to help defend it.

A PERSONAL ANECDOTE:

Jean-Pierre says he will never forget the reaction of an important client when he went to see him to announce a price reduction. The client's reaction was: "Absolutely not, it will destabilise the entire market." There aren't any other cultures where you'd get such a reaction. Though, obviously, this is less true when your business works on a sale-by-sale model such as capital equipment, machines, buildings.

8.1.4   Reputation and size of your company

Contrary to many other cultures, here, the reputation of your company (unless it's a bad one), your list of reference customers and the size of your company are not so important.

Often, 'small is beautiful' and young companies with novel approaches are very welcome. These societies tend to bubble with creativity and new products, and are ready to experiment with and develop new markets.

RECAP:

- Be prepared to negotiate a balanced win-win
- Be discrete: avoid a big car, dress simply but professionally, avoid ostentatiousness
- Be aware that within any given sector, everyone knows everyone

LIST OF CONNECTED COUNTRIES	Denmark, Estonia, Finland, Iceland, Latvia, Lithuania, Netherlands, Norway and Sweden

This cluster of countries is typified as Connected societies. In the table below, we have listed the scores of The Netherlands and Norway, as they are representative of this group of countries. You can add your own score or your home country's score in the last column.

	THE NETH-ER-LANDS	NOR-WAY	TYPICAL CHARACTERISTICS FOR THE CLUSTER	YOUR SCORE[10]
Power distance	35	31	Low	
Individualism	80	69	High	
Masculinity	14	8	Very low	
Uncertainty avoidance	53	50	Medium	
Long Term Orientation	67	35	Low to medium high	
Indulgence vs Restraint	68	55	Medium to high	

10 Please see page 38 on how to determine your own score.

8.2 The 6 steps of the sales process with the Connected

8.2.1 Establishing contact

The Connected are pretty egalitarian but also fairly closed. If you are not part of the network, you'll need to find a way to become part of it to be accepted. This is perfectly feasible but will require some time and effort. If a phone call doesn't result in the appointment you'd like, think about why that might be. Is the buyer aware that you are (or are not) known in her network? Or is she worried that you may present a challenge for an existing supplier? Don't give up; ask for a meeting just to get to know each other better.

What we are about to suggest would be utterly unacceptable in many cultures, but in The Netherlands, for instance, it is perfectly acceptable to call a prospective client and say something like: "I'll be in your area next week. Would it be possible to briefly drop by and have a chat over a coffee, just to get to know each other?"

Very quickly, the Connected tend to move on to a first name basis, but be careful about switching to this, especially with people older than you. Ask them first if it would be alright to do so, or, even better, wait until they suggest to do so themselves. Be aware of the delicate balance between formality and informality.

8.2.2 Establishing trust

If you are new to your counterpart, you may be surprised to find that she will have consulted your LinkedIn profile, your company website and asked around in her network about you. If your company is well known, you may need to explain why you didn't come and see her earlier, (be prepared to have a coherent story). In any case, you have work to do. Frequent contact by phone, email or visits will establish the relationship. Having a chat over coffee together is an important part of building the relationship. Conviviality is an essential element in the life of the Connected.

A COUPLE OF EXAMPLES:
The Dutch are big spenders when it comes to decorating their homes in order to make sure they are nice cosy places, well-suited to entertaining guests over coffee and cake.

Heineken's head office in Amsterdam has a tradition of free drinks and snacks at the company bar on Friday afternoon, after a long week of hard work. If you happen to be at their offices at the end of the working week, you are invited to join the crowd. The purpose is to improve the networking between diverse crowds of people in a relaxed atmosphere.

In several Scandinavian countries, it is normal to frequent the sauna with work colleagues as well as business partners. The relaxed atmosphere strengthens the development of a strong network inside as well as outside the company.

The Connected are often far more aware and conscious of differences between cultures. They probably know better than you do how your culture differs from theirs. Inviting a business partner out for lunch at a restaurant is quite unusual. Nevertheless, if you come from a culture where this is the norm, they'll be aware of that and graciously accept your invitation.

A PERSONAL ANECDOTE:

Marc had managed to secure an appointment with a new prospect (let's call him Olaf) in Denmark and they'd agreed to meet at 10 am. Murphy's Law would have it that Marc's plane was two hours delayed so he arrived at lunchtime. Marc called ahead and suggested that they have lunch together and do the introductions then. He asked Olaf to choose the restaurant. When Marc arrived at the office, they immediately left for the restaurant of Olaf's choice. They arrived there and it was closed. Olaf took them to another one, only to find that it was closed as well. Olaf became apologetic and explained that it was highly unusual to go out for lunch during a weekday and he was discovering with Marc that most restaurants were actually closed. In the end, they went to a major hotel in the area, hoping that their restaurant would be open. Fortunately, it was but they were the only guests. They had a very nice lunch and Olaf explained that he'd understood Marc's invitation, highly unusual as it may have been for him, because he'd worked for Danone for a while and was well aware of Marc's cultural norms. Actually, he very much appreciated the invitation and it laid the foundation for a very strong relationship. At the same time, it taught Marc that it might be more prudent to be less liberal with lunch invitations in that part of the world. He was keenly aware that not everyone might welcome such invitation the same way Olaf did.

8.2.3   Identifying the needs

For some of us, this conversation may be very surprising. Your counterpart will not hesitate at all to explain the strengths and weaknesses of his own company, and its market position, goals and expectations. He expects no less from you and will even want to know what you might consider to be confidential information or information that is not up to you to disclose. The conversation can either take the form 'this is what I need at this specific price' or, more generally, 'give me a couple of good reasons why our respective companies should start to collaborate'. Often, long meetings are necessary, but be confident – it certainly isn't a waste of time.

This step is probably the most pivotal one in the sales process, in the quest for a win-win. This is the time when each party hopefully discovers that the other has exactly that elusive missing piece to offer, which will be the basis for a highly successful partnership. Often marketing-oriented, the Connected buyer tends to be very well informed and will lead you into conversations that will require you to invest time and effort. It is not uncommon to be asked to present to a team of experts from logistics, production and even sales, so you can all debate together. The ultimate goal is always the quest for a long-term, win-win relationship.

Exchange information, discuss it in minute detail, build a close relationship, have a beer together, then go for a walk around the block while discussing the project because it's such a nice day and it would be a shame to waste it. All these are the building blocks for the relationship and help to determine the mutual needs that may unite you in a powerful partnership.

8.2.4   Presenting the commercial proposal

Depending on your counterpart, you'll need to gauge if the presentation needs to be formal or not. In any case, we recommend you make it an event. Ideally, one or two of your colleagues from logistics, marketing or R&D should accompany you so their counterparts can get to know them. This will be much appreciated.

Keep your presentation simple and factual, and make sure you're not over-selling. Be aware that we're in an environment which is, in many ways, the opposite of the highly masculine world of the Competitors. Over-selling, which is the norm for the Competitors, is regarded as ridiculous and blasé. The Dutch have a saying, *'Doe maar gewoon, dat is al gek genoeg'*, which translates roughly as: 'Just behave normally, that's already crazy enough'. This clearly illustrates their aversion to boasting and chest-beating.

Avoid too many extras or rebates in your proposal unless your counterpart specifically requested the offer be constructed like this. Once again, let's observe our car salesmen. Generally, you'll find a simple and clear all-in price, but there will be a couple of ways to reduce the price by removing one or more options. The Connected tend to be price sensitive, so building in room to negotiate the price downwards is advisable.

WHICH ARE THE ARGUMENTS THAT MAKE A DIFFERENCE?
Hofstede's scores will once again guide us in the choice of arguments. You'll want to dedicate enough time and effort to analyse and adapt your arguments and present them in an order which will satisfy the characteristics and needs of the Connected. The Connected typically like:
- Cooperation and consensus
- Innovation, initiative and risk-taking
- Ethical behaviour and social responsibility
- Quality of life

Back to our example of the watch. For the Connected, you need to use arguments that talk about the innovative aspects of the new design, the fact that the watch is made in a green factory using a manufacturing process that is eco-friendly and the exclusivity you're offering your counterpart for his region.

8.2.5   Negotiating the price

Usually, the price your customer needs will have been discussed whilst you were identifying the needs. She will probably have been quite clear with you what it needs to be, so there is not much final negotiation left. You might still throw in a bonus scheme or something else you deem useful to help shift the balance in your favour, but that's about it.
However, there's one last surprise in store for you.

8.2.6   Closing the deal

By now, you've understood that the Connected have a strong relationship with their suppliers. If you find yourself in a situation where you're replacing an existing supplier for a similar product or service, it is highly likely that your customer will ask for some understanding on your part because he needs to treat his current supplier correctly. This may mean that the current supplier will be informed of your conditions and given the opportunity to align with them. In other words, the current supplier has the opportunity to meet the conditions of the competition, and has a first right of refusal for the business. This may or may not be written in his contract but, for the Connected, it is such a normal part of a win-win relationship that he needs to go through what you might see as a divorce procedure.

As the new supplier, you may want to make sure that there's something unique in your value proposition which the existing supplier can't provide. It will significantly increase your chances of success. Note also that once you're in, it will be that much harder for a challenger to dislodge you as the relationship will now work in your favour.

RECAP:

- Plan enough time to develop a relationship and make sure it's solid
- Relationships are built between people but also between companies
- Remain true to your own culture, most likely they'll understand but be prepared to adapt your style of negotiation
- Be creative and invest time to find a win-win formula
- Communicate with the whole team

NEGOTIATING WITH THE CONNECTED

1	Establishing contact	A simple phone call may be enough. Insistence helps.
2	Establishing trust	Initially quite difficult to get to, the Connected is profoundly egalitarian. Be yourself and not the representative of your company. Be authentic. Trust will be established over time.
3	Identifying the needs	Ask a lot of questions, as the customer thinks he knows what he needs. You can start discussing the needs and open up the spectrum. Talk, discuss, and exchange lots of information.
4	Presenting the commercial proposal	The Connected will have helped you present the offer in way that works for him. No need for last minute 'wiggle room' – your proposal should reflect the final price.
5	Negotiating the price	Often, your price needs to correspond to the market price. Special conditions may be the key to success.
6	Closing the deal	If the relationship with the existing supplier is strong, he will be informed of your offer and given the opportunity to align his offering, to keep the business. It's the Connected's way of being fair with their partners. Remember, this also protects you once you're in.

CHAPTER 9

Mindset 4:

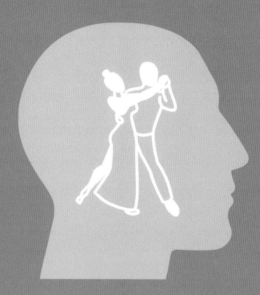

Negotiating with the 'Diplomat'

9

KEY WORDS: principals · hierarchy · philosophy · logic · structure · make sense · balance · respect · protocol · elegance · pragmatic · long term · serious · competitive

9.1   Why do we call them the Diplomats?

In our vocabulary, the Diplomat is very individualistic, highly respectful of hierarchy, dislikes open conflicts and is clearly uncomfortable with uncertainty. The concept of honour is an important driver for the Diplomat. France and Belgium are clear examples of this Diplomat mindset. For this group, the key to understanding them is, first of all, realising that they are not so easy to understand. On the one hand, they are very individualistic, but on the other, they have a strong hierarchy in their organisations. At first glance, this seems difficult to reconcile, but once you understand that they strongly dislike uncertainty, it is easier to understand why the strong hierarchy is there. Generally, they also tend to dislike open conflict and prefer to 'arrange' things.

We've chosen France as the reference country because it is better known around the world than Belgium. We're sure you can conjure up a picture of a 'typical' Frenchman in your mind. Maybe what you're about to read will reinforce that picture or it may give you new insights. At the minimum, it will help you to better understand the fundamentals of their negotiation style.

A few important pointers about the Diplomat's mindset before we dive in.

9.1.1   The perception of the organisation and relationship with authority

Almost every organisation is a pyramid with a clear hierarchy. The boss is always deferred to and nothing happens without the boss's seal of approval. Whilst Marc was growing up in Belgium, his parents sometimes cited the following Flemish saying: '*De baas is de baas al is het een mannetje van stro*', which means: 'The boss is the boss even if he's a straw puppet'. That says a lot, doesn't it?

You probably think that this doesn't gel with a highly individualistic character. Actually, it explains the never ending conflictual relationship the Diplomats have with authority. On the one hand, there is a clear respect and need for authority, but on the other, there are strong individualistic tendencies. This is the underlying reason why you see so many workers' strikes in France. It explains the disparity between the way an individual acts when he's with his superior, and how he acts when he's by himself or amongst peers.

9.1.2   The love of words

The diplomat is different from any other culture because of his conviction that words are much more than a mere tool of communication. Diplomats love the eloquent use of words and attribute a particular status to it. It is an integral and important part of their culture. In some other cultures, the content of the message is the most important (e.g. for the Competitors), while in others, one needs to be able to 'read the air', to carefully analyse body language as well as what is not said. For the French, the eloquent packaging of the message is just as important as the content of the message.

9.1.3   Deductive reasoning

The Diplomat prides himself on his deductive analytical thinking and his ability to develop all-encompassing models of the world. The way he builds an argument or explains something starts from the very big picture and slowly moves towards the topic which is of current concern.

To clarify, when he needs to explain the mechanism behind the tides of the sea, he'll start from the laws that govern the cosmos, then concentrate on the Milky Way, then our solar system and eventually the influence of the moon, all the time making sure that there is a logical progression from one step to the next.

This means that experts are highly rated. The white doctor's coat or the academic's title makes all the difference in the world. Evidence from laymen, perfectly acceptable in the Competitor's world, is much less valuable than information coming from an expert or academic.

9.1.4   The quest for elegance

The Diplomat is forever seeking elegance and beauty in his actions, his words, the systems he develops, and his surroundings. For those of you that are proficient in French, you know how 'flowery' the language is, especially in written form. The French take great pride in their 'language of Molière'. They consider themselves the owners of their language. The fact that they've set up L'Academie Française, whose sole purpose is to defend the French language, is a good indicator of this.

This quest for elegance also leads to an expectation of formality and style, both in behaviour and dress code.

Abroad, a Frenchman doesn't just represent himself or his company – he represents the French way of life, the French style and the French elegance. Let's not forget that the French are the inventors of modern diplomacy and have been practising it for centuries. We are talking about the art of establishing cordial relationships, of appropriate behaviour, of aligning everyone's interest and of obtaining commitments to further a common goal. Just think about the COP21, signed by 195 countries during a three-week climate summit in Paris. This was an achievement of epic proportions and testimony to the French art of diplomacy.

9.1.5   Fear of uncertainty

As a Belgian, it has taken Marc a while to get his mind around the idea that Belgian's score very highly on the uncertainty avoidance dimension. But after having moved to the UK, he has observed the striking difference in many aspects of life. Let us give you an example outside the commercial world but which illustrates the point very well:

In Belgium, the organisation of the school system is such that, until you enter university, everything is pre-arranged for you. Your schedule is clear and unambiguous. You're simply supposed to follow it. Most lessons take place in the same classroom and you'd only need to go to a different room for specialist topics that require a lab. It is not until you arrive at university that you are supposed to manage your own schedule and be on time at whichever location you need to be. And even then, each activity is carefully integrated into a schedule so there are never any conflicts.

When Marc's daughter was ten years old, his family moved to the UK and she entered a small boarding school. He was dumbfounded to find out that each topic had its own classroom, that there were a lot of scheduling conflicts between, for instance, music classes and science classes, that schedules changed all the time and that the kids were supposed to handle this on their own, showing up on time wherever they were supposed to be. It was not unusual for Marc's daughter to have to skip half of a class to be able to attend another. She was expected to juggle this, set her own priorities and catch up on missed lessons in her spare time. Marc really struggled to get his mind around the fact that this was NORMAL. The Brits don't feel that every detail needs to be carefully controlled and scheduled but are confident that overall, it will work fine. It is this experience which really made Marc understand that he does, in fact, come from a society which dislikes uncertainty much more than other societies.

9.1.6   The perception of French arrogance

As a French-Belgian, Jean-Pierre feels the need to elaborate on this subject because many negotiators complain about the "attitude of superiority" that the French exude in their interactions with foreigners. For people of this culture, this is not something conscious, but rather an unconscious awareness (if you'll forgive the oxymoron) amongst Latin people that they are the direct descendants and guardians of the Latin-Greek culture and mythology. They see it as the bedrock of the Western civilisation in which logical thinking, the art of philosophy and the discovery of many on the laws of nature are anchored. In Latin cultures, mythology is of prime importance for the education of modern man. In Greek and Latin mythology, the gods would punish man each time he deviated from the rules set out for him because in doing so, he endangered the cosmic order.

French education has remained very traditional in that its primary objective is to teach the 'art of logic' and the 'art of philosophy'. At eighteen, each young Frenchman must take a standard exam, called le BAC, and the very first part of it is 'the test of philosophy'. This shows the importance of philosophy in French society; even topics such as economy, science and technology are approached from a philosophical angle. The following are examples taken from real BAC exams:

Literature: "Is respecting each form of life a moral requirement?"
Economy: "Isn't the conscience of an individual simply a reflection of his society?"
Science: "Does politics require adherence to the principles of 'truth'?"
Technology: "Does culture define man?"

Because the French are taught to think in a deductive way, (e.g. from cosmic truths to practical issues), they find the opposite inductive way of working (e.g. solving practical issues by observing what works and developing best practices) almost too simplistic.

The French education instils in the French a sense that they understand the 'higher truths', while others may completely ignore them. This is the root of the perceived arrogance, and, hopefully, by being aware of it, you can enjoy the often very interesting philosophical conversations the French will encourage, rather than let them irritate you.

9.1.7   The 'grand écart'

The French have this 'easy' way of switching intellectually between opposing views – between the need to respect rules and the need to ignore them, between the respect for hierarchy and the need for individualism. They can perform this 'grand écart' without falling flat on their face.

9.1.8   Pragmatism nevertheless

After a lengthy introduction process, many back and forths, and potentially lengthy philosophical discussions about the right way to approach a market, your counterpart may surprise you by suddenly moving on to pricing, return on investment and growth. Many of the previously discussed challenges may simply disappear in view of the reality of life. Such is the pragmatic side of the Diplomat.

RECAP:

· Your counterpart probably doesn't have a mandate to make decisions
· Eloquence and the use of emotional words is appreciated
· Grand principles and philosophy rather than best practices
· Solutions should be elegant
· Rules are omnipresent
· Pragmatic nevertheless

LIST OF DIPLOMAT COUNTRIES	Belgium, France, Italy (North), Malta, Switzerland (Fr + It), Spain and Poland

This cluster of countries is typified as Diplomat societies. In the table below, we have listed the scores of France and Belgium in the Hofstede 6D model as they are representative of this group of countries. You can add your own score or your home country's score in the last column.

	FRANCE	BEL-GIUM	TYPICAL CHARACTERISTICS FOR THE CLUSTER	YOUR SCORE[11]
Power distance	68	65	Low	
Individualism	71	75	High	
Masculinity	43	54	Medium	
Uncertainty avoidance	86	94	High	
Long Term Orientation	63	82	High	
Indulgence vs Restraint	48	57	Low to medium	

11 Please see page 38 on how to determine your own score.

9.2 The 6 steps of the sales process with the Diplomats

9.2.1 Establishing contact

In a country that boasts founding concepts of freedom, equality and brotherhood (liberté, égalité et fraternité) you might think it would be easy to establish contact. It may surprise you that this is not the case. You'll find that it is not as complicated as in Asia but it isn't anywhere near as simple as in the USA. It might be easy if your company is very well known and/or prestigious, or if you are very well known yourself. But you probably don't represent Microsoft, and your name probably isn't Marc Zuckerberg, so you may find the following guidance useful:

DO YOUR HOMEWORK THOROUGHLY

Is your prospect already a customer of one of your direct competitors? What is the likelihood that she knows about you or your company? How is her organisation structured? Who leads the organisation? Is it possible to connect with someone at management level? Who is the ultimate decision maker? Who is the best person in the organisation to sell your proposal to?

Each bit of information you can glean will be useful to you.

INTRODUCTIONS GO A LONG WAY

Do you know someone who can and is willing to introduce you? You might think of asking around in your own network or use virtual networks such as LinkedIn to see which mutual connections you have. Maybe your embassy or consulate could help and organise a meeting for you? Is there a chamber of commerce that might be able to help you?

Being introduced to your prospect is the best possible way of establishing a successful contact, so we recommend you explore every possible option to achieve this.

WHAT IF YOU ARE UNABLE TO GET AN INTRODUCTION?

When you attempt to call your prospect, you will most likely reach an assistant. Your pitch to him will be crucial. Some examples of what you might want to say:

"I have been told that Mr Martin is in charge of logistics for your company. We have developed a new service and are looking for a partner in France."

"I understand your company is looking for... and we have developed a solution for another sector which might be of interest to you."

Maybe you'll be put through to the person you want to reach, or maybe you'll have to call back, perhaps even multiple times. Do NOT give up.

Some assistants may ask you to confirm the call by email. Assistants are important filters and hold a lot of power in their organisation's hierarchy so you'll need to be accommodating.

Do your best not to come across as someone who's merely prospecting but rather as someone that has done their homework and is convinced that they are bringing value to the organisation. Be aware that sales people are not held in high esteem by the Diplomats. They are stigmatised as the sort of people willing to sell their mother and father to reach their goal. In short, they are seen as untrustworthy. You may have noticed that the French rarely use the title 'vendeur' but instead use titles like 'Responsable Distribution' or 'Marketing Commercial' or even 'Ingénieur Commercial'. Titles like this take the focus off the commercial aspect of the job and show that the person has some kind of functional expertise that makes them more trustworthy.

If you can, tweak your title to make it sound as important as possible and minimise the reference to sales as much as possible.

9.2.2   Establishing trust

There you are at your first meeting and the diplomatic ballet has just started. Remain formal until your counterpart invites you to address her in a more informal way (e.g. by first name). If you are conducting the meeting in English, adjust your use of words and expressions to the Diplomat's level. The French are generally well educated, often able to read and write English well but are less comfortable speaking it. Keep this at the forefront of your mind to avoid misunderstandings.

'The customer is king' is a well-known French saying. Put your ego aside and start playing the game. You will have prepared your company presentation and ideally tailored it so that it has the most impact in the given situation. Maybe you have a second presentation exclusively dedicated to the product or service you wish to sell. It is quite possible that the first meeting will be solely dedicated to getting to know your company and judging if there is an interest in working with you. Remember the importance of a philosophical fit and for it to 'make sense' to work together. In France, one doesn't talk about the financial performance of one's company, the performance of its shares on the stock market or any other financial performance metric. Be aware that for the Diplomat, money is dirty and it is proper not to talk about it until one can no longer avoid the topic.

However, Diplomats love it if you talk about the size of the company in terms of number of people employed, or number of locations around the world. If your prospect employs 1,500 people, the impression you will make if your company employs 30,000 people will be very different from if it employs 500. In some cultures, this is irrelevant. Not so in France. If you are a start-up or an SME, focus on your impeccable service and flexibility, and accentuate the fact that you are 'on the ball'.

If the customer is important, attempt to schedule the meeting for 11 am. This will give you an opportunity to invite them for lunch. They may refuse the invitation, saying "next time, perhaps," but it is the 'right' thing to do.

Be guided by your counterpart throughout the meeting. Follow his or her rhythm, as this is the rhythm of the diplomatic ballet. Your main goals for this first meeting should be to:

- Make sure that your counterpart is sufficiently interested in or intrigued by what you have to offer.
- Have a clear understanding of your counterpart's position in the hierarchy and his decision-making authority. This is the key challenge in Latin cultures. You will have noted that France scores fairly high (68) on power distance dimension which signifies that it is a hierarchical society. At the same time, it scores high (71) on individualism. This may seem like a contradiction to you as in many parts of the world there is an inverse relationship between hierarchy and individualism. It is not easy to understand this contradiction, but it will be an important consideration in your negotiations. In France, even if your counterpart has what appears to be a clear title such as Purchasing Manager (Directeur des Achats), it doesn't automatically mean he has the authority to make the purchasing decision. Because of the importance of hierarchy, it is highly likely that the final decision will be made or will need to be approved by top management.

  Therefore, one way or another, in a very diplomatic manner, you need to find out how the final decision will be made and by whom. In other cultures, such as Organiser societies, this is a question that can simply be asked in a straightforward way. Not so with the French. We recommend gently approaching the subject in a more informal setting, perhaps over lunch or dinner, by asking questions like: "What is the decision-making process to switch supplier?" or "Who is part of the decision-making process?"

9.2.3   Identifying the needs

Congratulations. Reaching this stage means your counterpart has developed enough trust in you and your company to be able to move on to the next, more technical step. Ask a maximum of questions and let your counterpart express herself as freely as possible. Listen carefully because she'll express a range of technical and emotional needs. The truth is that the emotional needs can be more important than the technical ones. Fulfilling these is likely to make the ultimate difference between similar technical offerings. Make sure you understand her immediate needs as well as her long-term aspirations. Delay your formal presentation as long as possible so that you can tailor your arguments to her needs and thus maximise the impact.

Design your presentation in such a way that it flows from the big picture to the detailed solution. This approach will chime with the diplomat's tendency for deductive reasoning and feel right to her.

Don't be afraid to use big words and big ideas, but don't fall into the trap of over-selling, which is the norm with the Competitors. The key is an eloquent and articulate use of the right words and the big ideas. Think about the philosophical aspect of your activity. What does it mean for human relationships, for society at large? Your business needs, somehow, to 'make sense'. It is important to identify some form of elegance about your offering, be it technical, intellectual or ecological, prior to knuckling down to the nitty-gritty of economic benefits, pricing, etc.

The French are always looking for elegance. It could be the fact that this new generation of packaging machine has the elegance of reducing energy costs and saving raw materials, whilst improving technical performance. Your IT solution can have the elegance of logic and simplicity. Your logistics solution will help to reduce inventory and as such 'makes sense', because it reduces energy consumption. The more your service or product is intellectually and emotionally interesting and stimulating, the better your chances of closing the deal will be.

9.2.4   Presenting the proposal

Always remember that talking about money is not dignified for a Diplomat [12]. The tradition of making a formal written offer is firmly anchored in the French culture. This helps to avoid having to talk too much about price. Nevertheless, in our experience, there is space for some discussion of price. Ask questions such as: "In order to meet your requirements, I think we'll end up around this price. Does that seem acceptable to you?" Pay close attention to the Diplomat's reaction. Is he relieved that you have broached the subject? Do you get a frank and honest answer? Or does he remain vague? Most of the important points, such as the market price, will have been discussed in the previous phase but rarely will you have discussed specifics, like what he currently pays for a certain service or product. If you choose to ask this question, make sure you observe his body language too. You will most likely see how uncomfortable the question is for your counterpart.

We recommend you make a formal written offer that takes everything you've discussed and learned up to now into account. This will be a very important basis for your relationship. It will be the 'bible' which will serve as the reference point for

---

12 In the Roman Mythology, Mercury was the god of merchants, commerce but also the god of the thieves. This suggest that the two go hand in hand. https://simple.wikipedia.org/wiki/Mercury_(mythology)

the future of your relationship. Every detail of past conversations should be included, but we recommend that you conveniently 'forget' a few that don't suit you. Add a few extra features at additional cost but do not mention any bonuses. This will be useful when the real price negotiation commences. Make sure you keep a sufficient margin for negotiation because it is very likely that your first offer will be rejected, as a matter of principal. This is a normal tactic which really serves internal politics, so the buyer can show his usefulness to the organisation. Remember, you are not negotiating with the Competitors or the Organisers who would not appreciate a diplomatic ballet. Rest assured that you will have an opportunity to make a second, improved offer. It's all part of the game.

WHICH ARE THE ARGUMENTS THAT MAKE A DIFFERENCE?
Looking at Hofstede's country scores for the Diplomats, you will find excellent guidance. Make sure you present the arguments in the order of importance they have for your counterpart.

Diplomats like (and need):
- Security and reliability (high uncertainty avoidance)
- Discreet elegance
- The long-term view
- A solid foundation and sense-making

Therefore, if you're selling a new concept for a watch, you should emphasise the fact that the combination of features of this product makes sense, the life-long warranty, the exceptionally elegant design, the fact that its lack of batteries makes it more environmentally friendly and the logic of the technological advances.

9.2.5   Negotiating the price

This is a sensitive and delicate moment. Remember, money is dirty and talking about is perceived as degrading. It just isn't an appropriate topic for Diplomats. It is an unavoidable discussion, but Diplomats want to spend as little time on it as possible. That's why many companies have a dedicated buyer. Many times, both of us have reached this stage and been told that everything looks very promising, only to find we now need to meet with the buyer, who is effectively the mean guy on the block. If there is no dedicated person, your contact may take on the role himself and you may discover a whole different side of his personality entering this phase of the negotiation with you.

French professional buyers have a reputation for being very tough. We have been told that one of the reasons why Carrefour, Sodexo and Accor hotels have become so successful globally is because of their ability to create an impressive buying power, using a distinctly un-French (perhaps 'inelegant') approach.

You have now entered a chapter which may take quite some time, during which the price must be reduced. Be aware of this and make sure you have a margin for negotiation that is appropriate for your industry and your market. It is in France that we discovered the term 'apparent market price'. Clearly, the market price does not equal the best price, so bonuses on various levels (quantity, corporate, etc.) will be necessary. The Diplomat always needs to negotiate so be prepared.

Confronted with the buyer, you can use France's hierarchical approach to your advantage and say that you do not have the authority to finalise the price. This way, you can play the role of a go-between who will do his best to arrive at a deal. This often allows for a more open, less emotional conversation with the buyer and may provide you with extra insight. It also allows you to send strong messages such as: "There is no point in presenting your request or position to my top management because I know upfront they will refuse." It allows you to be in control without appearing to be so.

9.2.6   Finalising the deal

This phase depends a lot on how well you've prepared the terrain. If you have managed to connect with and convince all the people involved in the decision-making process (logistics, finance, technical, operations and management), and none of them have vetoed anything then all will most likely be well. The most difficult group to anticipate is often top management. They remain mysterious and will not share their decision-making process with you. It is very typical for top management in a hierarchical organisation to maintain a certain degree of neutrality which allows them to decline a deal even if the entire team supports it. The entire organisation understands and accepts this, which is why it is crucial for you to establish a good relationship with each person that is involved in the process, so that they may tell you what you need to do to conclude the deal. Some will help you, explaining that they favour the conclusion of a deal with you, and they may let you know that their colleague X or Y still needs some convincing. If you've established a really good relationship, they'll even tell you what you need to do and how you need to do it to increase your chances of success.

At this point, the deal is as good as yours, but there is one last detail to be aware of. Contrary to some other cultures, the Diplomats have clearly defined ethical standards that do not allow them to share your proposal with your competitors. However, this rule is not always respected. If someone in the organisation likes your offer but would prefer to stick with their current supplier, she may leak your conditions and allow the incumbent supplier to align his offer with your proposal. You need to keep this in mind all the time and protect yourself as best as you can.

RECAP:

· Collect as much information about your prospect as possible
· Get introduced
· Prepare your pitch to show off your knowledge of their company
· Be patient and persistent
· Make sure you adjust your use of the English language to the language level of your counterpart
· The customer is KING: be patient
· Be prepared with presentations but don't show them until asked
· Attempt to understand the decision-making authority of your counterpart

NEGOTIATING WITH THE DIPLOMATS

1	Establishing contact	An introduction is ideal. If not possible, a simple phone call may be enough. Don't hesitate to call multiple times. Personal or company reputation or a title are helpful.
2	Establishing trust	Hierarchy is important. Make sure you meet people who are at least at the same level as you. If possible, meet with the higher-ups in the organisation. References, common connections, etc. will help. Do NOT talk about money and price at this stage.
3	Identifying the needs	Expect and prepare for sophisticated conversation in which philosophy is important. Use a deductive approach starting from the big picture down to the details. Use sentences such as "What if we could help you with...?" "Would it make sense if...?"
4	Presenting the commer-cial propos-al	Indispensable highly detailed and formal document describing the content as well as the price. Make sure you have wiggle-room for further negotiation. Use arguments built on reliability, elegance, discretion and intelligence. Follow up with a call or a visit.
5	Negotiating the price	A second round will be necessary. Use the sense of hierarchy to play the diplomatic ballet.
6	Closing the deal	Being competitive is not enough to secure the order. Top management has the last say and may wish to stick with the current supplier. If needed, a meeting between top management on both sides might work magic. Make sure to keep room to negotiate until the last moment.

CHAPTER 10

Mindset 5:

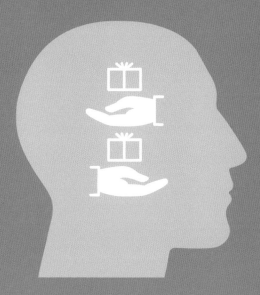

Negotiating with the 'Reciprocator'

10

KEY WORDS: group-focus · hierarchy · harmony · loyalty · honour · relationship · respect · indirect communication · formalism · procedures · saving face

10.1 Why do we call them the Reciprocators?

Reciprocator societies are formed of groups whose interactions, both within and between the groups, are based on exchanging or reciprocating favours, or helping each other out.

In our vocabulary, we characterise these societies as collectivist, very much hierarchical, avoidant of open conflicts and disliking uncertainty. Honour is a key factor in their behaviour. Organised in groups that either compete or cooperate, they influence each other, which ultimately leads to a pyramid structure of groups that form the society. If you are from an individualist culture, you may first want to read chapter 13.3 to get some insight into the importance of relationships for this group. They will be an important key to your success.

We have chosen Morocco to illustrate the group of the Reciprocators. We will handle this chapter as if we were going to explore the Moroccan market together.

A few important pointers about the Reciprocator's mindset before we dive in:

10.1.1   It's all about exchanging favours

'You do something for me, I'll do something for you' is the overall principle that guides life in this cluster. A friend of ours once shared his experience of doing business in Russia. Getting your invoices paid can be a real issue. After our friend had chased a payment from a customer for quite some time, the customer finally paid, but then expected our friend to be grateful for the 'favour' he'd done him by paying the invoice. Furthermore, the customer now expected a reciprocal favour from our friend.

Another example from a different aspect of life comes from refugee integration. Working with the Red Cross, Marc was told that whenever a refugee family was assigned permanent accommodation by the authorities in their host country, the typical reaction of other families on the waiting list was: "What were the favours exchanged so this family got their accommodation?" For them, every transaction had to be an exchange of favours, so they couldn't imagine that the assignment of accommodation was simply the end result of following a process and procedures.

10.1.2   The rituals and customs

At the risk of repeating ourselves, we want to emphasise how important it is that you inform yourself about the rituals, customs and traditions of the country you are going to visit. There are dozens of books that deal with this subject for any country you might visit, so it's a good idea to do some reading before your first interactions. However, as long as you are genuinely trying to be polite and respectful, the occasional mistake or a bit of ignorance will be accepted and forgiven and will not negatively impact your relationship.

There are some famous awkward pictures of Barack Obama trying to give a hug to Aung San Suu Kyi and George Bush trying to hug Mrs. Lin Piao, but they are not the diplomatic disaster one might imagine. They are simply funny because in these cultures, one doesn't touch one another. It is always better to be aware but one shouldn't exaggerate either. In trying too hard to adapt, one may come across as a little bit weird. You will never be able to get it a hundred percent right and your hosts will realise that you are just aping them. However, they will appreciate it if you treat their business card with respect, don't write anything on it, read it carefully and store it nicely. They appreciate it if you look them in the eyes whilst greeting them. In some countries, one doesn't smile and in others one smiles a lot. The Reciprocators find politeness and thoughtfulness very important. They have a lot of customs and rituals and the degree to which one adheres to them is an indication of how well one was raised and educated.

10.1.3   Hierarchy and decision making

In the Reciprocator's world, decisions are made at the top and the rest of the organisation executes them unquestioningly. Bosses and elders are deferred to because of their position, not necessarily because of their knowledge, experience or expertise. Powerholders, and thus decision-makers, can be relatively easily recognised by strong symbols of power.

10.1.4   Favoritism and Loyalty

In this collectivist world, which seeks to avoid and control uncertainty, it is entirely logical for a business leader to surround himself with people he knows and trusts, can control and for whom he is responsible. Do not underestimate the importance and normality of this, even if you find it hard to deal with.

10

RECAP:

- · First establish a good relationship
- · Think in terms of exchanging favours
- · Study the rituals and customs
- · Respect for hierarchy
- · The interest of the group is more important than the interest of the individual

LIST OF RECIPROCATOR COUNTRIES	East Africa, West Africa, Middle East, Albania, Angola [13], Argentina, Bangladesh [13,] Brazil, Bulgaria, Burkina Faso [13], Cape Verde, Chili, Colombia, Costa Rica, Croatia, Ecuador, Egypt, El Salvador, Ethiopia [13], Ghana, Greece, Guatemala, Honduras, Iran, Iraq, Jordan [13], Kenya, Kuwait, Libya, Lebanon, Malawi, Mexico, Morocco, Mozambique, Nigeria [13], Pakistan, Panama, Peru, Portugal, Romania, Russia, Saudi Arabia, Senegal [13], Serbia, Sierra Leone, Slovakia, Slovenia, South Korea Suriname, Syria [13], Taiwan, Tanzania, Thailand [13], Trinidad, Turkey, UAE, Uruguay, Venezuela, Zambia

We have typified this cluster of countries as Reciprocator societies because their main mode of operation is the exchange of favours. In the table below, we have listed the scores of Morocco and Russia in the Hofstede 6D model as they are representative of this group of countries. You can add your own score or your home country's score in the last column.

---

13 These countries have a score of 50 on the dimension of Uncertainty Avoidance. We decided to classify them as Reciprocators but you will also find a Marathonian mindset there.

	MO-ROCCO	RUSSIA	TYPICAL CHARACTERISTICS FOR THE CLUSTER	YOUR SCORE[14]
Power distance	70	93	High	
Individualism	46	39	Low	
Masculinity	53	36	Medium	
Uncertainty avoidance	68	95	High	
Long Term Orientation	14	81	N/A	
Indulgence vs Restraint	25	20	N/A	

10.2 The 6 steps of the sales process with the Reciprocators

In the world of the reciprocator, negotiation is not a linear process as it is in most of the western world. A negotiation can take a long time and the steps may be revisited regularly. Also, the distinction between them can be quite blurred and not nearly as clear and distinct as we have seen in the previous chapters.

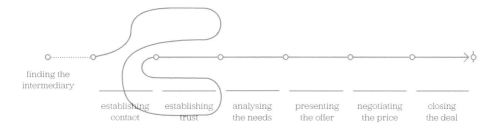

finding the intermediary — establishing contact — establishing trust — analysing the needs — presenting the offer — negotiating the price — closing the deal

10.2.1   Establishing contact

There is no point in trying to establish contact with a potential customer without having used your own network or having enlisted the help of a trade-promotion agency to establish contact with one or more commercial intermediaries who can,

14 Please see page 38 on how to determine your own score.

in turn, introduce you to potential clients. The key to understanding this is that, here, 'the friends of my friends are also my friends'. Any Moroccan within your own network, provided he has the relevant socio-cultural background, will perfectly understand and be happy to help you with introductions. Let's say that during a family holiday in Tangiers, you had the occasion to meet the owner of the small family hotel you were staying in. You spent a good amount of time with him and your family remembers him fondly. He was very charming, kind and clearly well-educated. Find his email address or phone number and contact him. After a bit of small talk reminding him of the good time you had together, you can easily continue the conversation as follows: "I'll be back in your beautiful country shortly to explore the market for my plumbing products. Unfortunately, I don't have any contacts and I was wondering if you might have any recommendations for me." Stanley Milgram, a well-known American social psychologist, conducted the 'small-world' experiment and found that, in the US, any person is connected to any other person by five intermediaries on average (i.e. six degrees of separation). We'd be very surprised if you'd need that many in a collectivist country such as Morocco.

So, one contact will recommend another one, and you'll end up meeting with the third who might not be a distributor of plumbing materials but tells you he has an excellent relationship with the most important distributor in the region. You'll probably need to court him a bit before you'll be able to get to his connections but don't underestimate the potential. It will be helpful if you discreetly convey the message that, in case you manage to successfully develop business thanks to his help, you may be able to help him as well. Maybe you know someone in your network that might help him? Maybe you can do so yourself? In this world, reciprocating favours is the glue of society and is much more valuable than money.

10.2.2 Establishing trust

Congratulations, you managed to secure a meeting. Now you're in front of a businessman, who is likely to be a bit more individualistic than his typical fellow countrymen. He'll probably introduce you to his son-in-law or his cousin as his right-hand man.

You'll need to be very patient, spend time drinking lots of tea with them, learn about all the things that occupy and worry them in their day-to-day lives and learn how you can connect with them by understanding what motivates and drives them. Conversation will invariably be implicit. They may talk about the fact that the mayor, who lives in the big mansion at the end of the road, is well connected to the patrons of the Casablanca stock exchange, who in turn are well connected the Minister of Economy. You are expected to talk about your successes, the status of your customers, etc. These conversations will establish reputation and trust.

A PERSONAL ANECDOTE:

Peter, a white Zimbabwean living in South-African, who runs a motorcycle business once told us the following story. He had a business idea to close the last mile between the end of the public transport system and the homes of people in rural areas, using a motorcycle service. His normal approach would have been to go and sell the concept and the benefits it could bring to the rural population, building on some kind of cost/benefit analysis. Moses, his second in command and a black South-African, organised several meetings with village elders to see if the idea was viable. He instructed Peter very clearly that, apart from introducing the basic idea, there was not to be any talk about business at all during the first meeting. He was hardly expected to say anything while Moses conducted most of the conversation. And indeed, the first meeting was all about establishing who Peter was, who his parents were, why he had come to South Africa, etc. The meeting ended with the elders saying they'd think about the idea and get back to him. It took a second meeting with hardly any business talk before enough trust was established to finally start talking business.

10.2.3 Identifying the needs, presenting the commercial proposal and negotiating the price

Of course, you'll have already identified the needs of your counterpart during the long tea-drinking sessions you've had and they will very likely not correspond to your standard offering or standard approach. But actually, that isn't necessarily very important in a culture where relationships are as important as the actual product. Reciprocators are not interested in buying your product just for its characteristics, specifications and price but rather because of the strength of your relationship, the warranties you offer and the exclusivity of your relationship. Remember that just yesterday, over a cup of tea, you were asked if, by any chance, you happened to know someone who specialised in supplying LED light fixtures. Such a question may seem a bit strange coming from a distributor of plumbing materials but know that in reality he was probably testing the extent of your network.

Reciprocator culture is one where talking about money is difficult and feels a bit dirty. Your counterpart may find it hard to ask you for the price. If you want the play the game to the max, then, with a dismissive wave of your hand, you can reply something like: "In any case, if we have the pleasure of working together, we'll corner the whole market. By combining the power of your distribution network with our productivity, we'll be very competitive. Let's see if we can build a strong partnership by agreeing on a strategy that works for both of us first."

A PERSONAL ANECDOTE:

Jean-Pierre once assisted at a negotiation in Indonesia. The European buyer told the Indonesian seller what price he'd paid the previous month for a certain product. The seller explained that unfortunately he would have to ask twice that price. Jean-Pierre obviously was very interested in the arguments the seller was going to use to justify his positioning. "That particular competitor is specifically equipped to produce the product at high volume and low cost," he explained. "The quantities I am selling are far smaller so therefore my cost price is much higher and I have no choice but to ask a higher price." They ended up compromising but the seller never even considered the buyer might choose not to do the transaction. He was convinced they were going to buy from him and shared his problem with them openly.

Think about the logic of this transaction which is entirely different from what one encounters in individualist societies. In the seller's mind, the deal was done because they had established a climate of trust. It would be unheard of, not to say dramatic, to fail to come to an agreement at this stage. This is why the previous stage, the establishment of trust, is so important.

WHICH ARE THE ARGUMENTS THAT MAKE A DIFFERENCE?
Once again, the Hofstede scores will guide you in your choice of arguments. You'll want to prepare and arrange your arguments in an order which takes the expectations of your counterpart into account.
Moroccans like:
- A stable relationship
- Loyalty
- Harmony
- Safety and reliability
- Formality
- Hierarchy

So back to our concept of selling a new watch, you'll need to emphasise the lifetime warranty, the fact that it is made by experts (invite them to visit the factory), the prestige it offers (one might even offer it to a government minister), and the advantages there are to possessing one.

You'll be able to deal with this step quite comfortably because the proposal will be the reflection of a whole series of conversations you'll have had before. But still, this is a necessary step and a subject for discussion. Give yourself enough margin to manoeuvre along a path of logic you'll have carefully prepared before. You can and may have to lower your price, but always in exchange for some kind of compensation or concession. Think about how the Moroccan car sales manager presents the price of a car. Quite often, you won't even find a displayed price, and finding it out will require long conversations and additional bits of information.

10.2.4   Closing the deal

You need to carefully consider what the best approach is in a market that puts more value on the quality of the relationship than on the price or the quality of the product.

OBTAINING THE ORDER

Very often, you'll need something to force the final decision. It could be an out-of-stock situation, or an urgent order of another very important customer (a government minister, a king...). But it should be something which is not easily resolved and helps to accelerate the decision-making process.

You may find it difficult to orchestrate such event. You can try strategies like offering extra inventory that needs to be got rid of, special pricing, or the need for you personally to show results quickly, but be careful because if you're not a master at the game, you may easily be found out by the experts that Reciprocators are.

10

- Spend time with your counterpart
- Avoid going by yourself, think of taking someone along
- Work hard at establishing a relationship of trust and loyalty
- Business is done with friends

NEGOTIATING WITH THE RECIPROCATORS

1	Establishing contact	The contact will be established by one or a series of intermediaries or common friends, which will establish the beginnings of trust.
2	Establishing trust	Trust is established on a person to person basis. Acceptance in the circle of trust depends on you personally. During your visit, avoid talking about business but rather spend time getting to know one another.
3	Identifying the needs, presentation of the offer and negotiation of the price	Identifying the needs, presentation of the offer (or estimate) and negotiation of the price are all part of one integrated conversation. Both parties try to find out what might be of interest for the other party. "If I give you this, and you give me that then we're both happy." It is really difficult and painful to change existing relationships. Spend enough time to make time.
4	Closing the deal / re-negotiating the price	Finally, one day, the deal will be closed because you have established the relationship, you trust one another and have found a win-win situation.

Mindset 6:

Negotiating with the 'Marathonian'

11

KEY WORDS: hierarchy · loyalty · rules · centralisation · flexibility · pragmatism · indirect communication · saving face

11.1 Why do we call them the Marathonians?

Unlike the groups we've seen before, that mostly see a negotiation as a linear process, for this group, it is much more like a never-ending circle of negotiation and renegotiation.

Never make the mistake of thinking that you are negotiating with an autonomous individual, but rather keep in mind that you are negotiating with one part of a bigger entity.

In our vocabulary, we characterise the mindset of the Marathonians as collectivist, very respectful of hierarchy and power, driven by ambition, success and recognition, and completely at ease with uncertainty. We'll find most of these societies in the Far East but also a few in the Caribbean.

Since many readers will have to work with China sooner or later, we'll base this chapter on China as the reference country for this group.

Before we dive in deeper, we'd like to dispel several clichés and misconceptions.

11.1.1 Intellectual property

You've probably heard about the disregard the Chinese have for intellectual property rights.

> A PERSONAL ANECDOTE:
>
> *When Jean-Pierre was visiting his son in China, his son, after just two phone calls, managed to obtain a list of the top 500 companies in Beijing with detailed contact information (name and telephone numbers) of their HR directors, with the help of his Chinese friend. As Jean-Pierre wanted to understand how this friend had been able to obtain all this information, he asked his son to organise a meeting with her. It turned out to be a very interesting experience for him.*
>
> *They talked about the concept of ownership and Jean-Pierre explained to her that in his mind, his own contact information which he had just*

*given her, had become her property. As far as he was concerned, she owned the contact information on that piece of paper and, if she compiled an address list, it was **her** list. Having this conversation with her helped him to understand her point of view but also made him realise the peculiarity of his own perspective on ownership. Her perspective could be summarised as follows: "I don't feel that contact information is my property and therefore I don't feel I own that list either." Jean-Pierre pointed out to her that she had worked to compile that list and that it could now save time and be valuable for a competitor. She answered him as follows: "It was your son who asked me to compile that list, not just anyone, and he explained to me that you were not competing with me, so I was happy to help."*

We can learn two important things from this anecdote. First, Chinese culture respects ownership but conceptually, ownership can only be physical in nature. Ownership of, say, a car, a home, or a watch is respected because these are physical objects. The virtual side of ownership, of things such as intellectual property, is viewed differently and you'll be hard pressed to explain that an idea can be owned by someone.

11.1.2   Reciprocating favours

From the previous anecdote, we also learn that, in China, it is important to help each other, and to reciprocate favours. That is a person's true wealth and currency. The more people owe you, the more important you are and, potentially, the richer you are. This is one of the key concepts to really understanding the mindset of collectivist cultures, and is indispensable for establishing personal relationships, which form the basis for good business.

For individualists, a sales transaction is the exchange of money for a product or a service. In a collectivist country, a sales transaction is the exchange of a series of favours. You'll supply something above and beyond your product or service. Maybe you can help the Marathonian gain status in his group by inviting him to your home country to visit your factory of offices or by enabling him to invite his family or friends for dinner. It's your job to find out what it is that enhances your counterpart's status in his group and find a way to make it happen.

A consequence of all this is that signed contracts are not all that important. A purchase order will be signed easily, because in the end it's only a piece of paper which will be reviewed and re-assessed at every turn of events. Don't count on finding a court in any of these countries that will be hold someone accountable to a piece of paper.

11.1.3   Asian finesse

Often, the games of 'chess' and 'go' are used to explain the differences between Eastern and Western cultures. In the context of negotiation, this comparison will be useful. What am I talking about? In chess, each piece has its own numeric value and the highest of the sum of those numeric values will lead to victory. Therefore, whilst playing the game, one carefully protects each individual piece and only gives one up if one can capture an equivalent one. The game of go is more strategic. One can easily afford to lose a couple of pieces if it leads to a tactical advantage on the playing field.

During negotiations, the Chinese tend to adopt a bird's-eye perspective and are not overly worried about conceding a few points, as long as equilibrium is maintained. You need to be aware that Marathonians will not disclose their real priorities to you, and even enjoy leading you down the garden path to achieve a tactical advantage. The book 'The Art of War', written by general Sun Tzu in the 6th Century BC, is still very popular. It consists of thirteen chapters, each of which describe a different aspect of warfare, and is considered the definitive work on military tactics and strategies of its time. Sun Tzu describes a whole series of deceptions and tactics, such as how to feign weakness, surprise your enemy, or lose a small battle, all to make sure that you win the war in the end. Add to that the strong cultural desire to avoid losing face, which makes a direct approach undesirable, and you start to understand that for the Chinese, the art of negotiation is a series of apparently innocuous conversations and allusions, rather than direct analysis and decision. If you're from an individualist society, you may feel that nothing is moving forward.

11.1.4   Chinese consumers and their relationship with the rest of the world

China's relationship with the West is changing. On the one hand, when you browse through some Chinese high-life magazines, you'll see that the fashion products are usually Western and that almost all the models are Eurasian or even clearly Western. In 2014, Marc visited a big mall in Shanghai and, apart from the people in it and some of the restaurants, nothing would have indicated that he was actually in China. Looking at the shops and the publicity, you might just as well have been in a mall in London, New York or Paris. On the other hand, at the time of writing of this book, Chinese consumers are becoming more and more proud of their home-made products, especially for high tech items such as smartphones. Owning a strong Western brand used to be enough to be successful in China. As Chinese consumers are becoming more confident in the quality of their own products, it is increasingly harder for Western brands to develop their market in China [15].

11.1.5   The age of the little emperors

Although China is a very collectivist society, we are possibly beginning to see a surface-level shift, of which the consequences, on a sociological level, are yet to be researched. Because of the one-child policy, which allowed most of the Chinese families to have only one child, most of today's young adults grew up without siblings. Growing up with siblings teaches you to compromise and rubs off your sharp corners from a social perspective. Since a generation of parents only had one child, no effort was spared to look after each child's wellbeing and many children were spoiled. This age group is known as 'The Little Emperors', who are used to always getting things their way without having to compromise. This may cause the collectivist nature of the Chinese society to shift towards more individualism. Only time will tell how this might effect this core value, but it is good to be aware of this and to be prepared.

15. Source: NIELSEN 2014 report 'What will consumers buy next' presented to LBS students in Shanghai

- The concept of ownership relates to physical goods only
- Relationships are more important than contracts
- Winning the war is more important than winning the battle
- Increasing importance of home-made goods
- Building trust is not easy
- Beware of the potential impact of the one child policy

LIST OF MARATHONIAN COUNTRIES	Bhutan, China, Dominican Republic, Fiji, Hong Kong, India, Indonesia, Jamaica, Malaysia, Namibia, Nepal, The Philippines, Singapore, Sri Lanka, Vietnam

We have typified this cluster of countries as Marathonian societies because their main mode of operation is never ending loops of negotiation and renegotiation. In the table below, we have listed the scores of China and India on the Hofstede 6D model as they are two of the world's biggest economies and representative of this group of countries. Looking at the scores, you can see that India is more individualist and less long term oriented than China. You can add your own score or your home country's score in the last column.

	CHINA	INDIA	TYPICAL CHARACTERISTICS FOR THE CLUSTER	YOUR SCORE[16]
Power distance	80	77	High	
Individualism	20	48	Low to medium	
Masculinity	66	56	Medium to high	
Uncertainty avoidance	30	40	Low	
Long Term Orientation	87	51	Medium to high	
Indulgence vs Restraint	24	26	Low to medium	

16 Please see page 38 on how to determine your own score.

11.2 The 6 steps of the sales process with the Marathonians

11.2.1 Establishing contact

By now you know that there is no point in trying to contact a Chinese person that you don't know. It is absolutely indispensable for you to find a commercial intermediary. It may cost you a bit, especially if you use a private sector service provider. You may want to use your local government agency that provides help and assistance for export related matters. They will be able to find the right intermediary or introduce you directly to one or more contacts. Insist on a personal introduction by them as it will make all the difference in the world. The quality and level of the introduction will determine the quality of your relationship and the success of your venture. Economising on this step, almost regardless of the cost, would really result in a complete loss of time, effort and money. At this stage, finding the right intermediary is your primary objective. It will not be easy as you'll need to make sure that she's competent and has the network you need. This is where your adventure starts, because, as time goes by, the intermediaries are becoming more and more professional themselves and tend to be very good negotiators.

AN ANECDOTE FROM A FRIEND:

Before she became a digital project manager at a Chinese company, Angela used to work for an Australian company that focused on foreign brands entering the Chinese market. When she joined the Chinese company, her senior manager gave her a list of contacts, stating "These people are part of our company's "network", some of them are my personal friends, try to take contact with them first, chat, invite them for tea and try to befriend them, this way you will sign your first contract very soon!

Angela was a bit confused about this approach, but she did what her senior manager had advised. To her surprise, soon one of the person on the contact list introduced her to a client, and she landed her first deal.

After working as project manager for more than one year, Angela found it was extremely hard to reach a client directly. Intermediaries and common acquaintances made everything much easier. A lot of her clients were introduced by her former clients, most of them are friends of friends. As a project manager, one of the most important capacity is to be able to keep a good relationship with clients and intermediary. They are the key for you to establish contact.

In conclusion, invest the necessary effort, time and money to integrate in existing networks, find the common acquaintances or find the intermediary with the right set of contacts. In case you use an intermediary, always be conscious of the fact that he is your most important asset and integrate him in your group. Make sure you understand the customs and rituals as well as the limits of what may be asked of you.

Don't feel as if you should know it all or behave as if you do. A French friend of ours who speaks perfect mandarin told us that despite his mastery of the language, he never visits a customer without being accompanied by a native Chinese speaker. It's not just the language. There are so many unwritten and unfamiliar rules in the personal relationships between the Chinese that you can't ever be sure to understand it all.

11.2.2 Establishing trust

If you've managed to find a good intermediary, this step shouldn't be too difficult. Don't get us wrong, you still have to work hard to accomplish this successfully. There are no shortcuts. Essentially, the prospects you were introduced to by your intermediary will be favourably inclined towards you, but that is not enough. Don't be surprised if you don't receive a warm welcome, because Chinese culture requires emotional control and an expressionless face. Westerners tend to think that when communicating with foreign people, facial expressions need to be amplified – a broader smile, or eyebrows used a bit more forcibly, for example.

AN ACCOMPLISHED BUSINESS MAN (LET'S CALL HIM TOM)
ONCE SHARED THE FOLLOWING ANECDOTE WITH US:

 Soon after graduating, Tom was put in charge of the legal department of a major German pharmaceutical company. He was sent to China to assist the project manager who was in the preparation phase for the construction of a new production facility. They had planned a five-day trip to meet with the authorities, the contractors and the architects of the project. Their schedule, organised by their intermediary, included three or four meetings a day, which should have allowed them to significantly advance with the project. The first meeting was with the local mayor. They arrived in good time, having been driven there by their intermediary. They were received by a friendly Chinese man who served them tea. It took them half an hour to realise that he was not the mayor of the town, but an assistant whose role they never quite understood. They looked to their intermediary for clarification but he seemed quite at ease with the situation. They, on the other hand, were becoming quite nervous, as time was passing by and they were obviously not achieving anything. They'd been through all the meaningless conversations and once they all knew how many children each person had, and what their names and ages were, they became quite impatient and started to show it. The intermediary took them aside and explained that the schedule which they had imposed on him could never work and that they were going to have to spend at least two days meeting different people of the town's administration alone. The project manager nodded slightly as a signal to Tom and they accepted the intermediary's recommendations with a big smile. They ended up drinking tea non-stop for five days, making long lists of names and putting them in organisational charts. Young and inexperienced as Tom was, he was champing at the bit, but in hindsight, he knows that the project manager was right. They constantly adapted to the requirements of the ritual and in the end the whole project was a big success.

This step is absolutely crucial and, going forward, if you make little mistakes, as you undoubtedly will, you'll be easily forgiven if you showed yourself to be flexible and adaptable in the beginning of the process. You do not need to worry about being viewed as a 'soft' negotiator, as might happen in other cultures. On the contrary, you will be seen as having been well advised and you will be respected all the more for it.

11.2.3 Identifying the needs, presenting the offer, negotiating the price and concluding the deal

The identification of the needs, presentation of the offer and negotiation of the price are all bundled up in one big step because, for this group, it is not a linear process, but rather a rotating spiral that slowly spins, constantly morphs, and expands or contracts depending on the situation. Don't be surprised during this phase if subjects you thought were fully handled and taken care of are suddenly revisited by your counterpart, because nothing is ever fixed but rather relative to context and timing. If your own cultural profile fits that of the Diplomat's, you shouldn't have too much trouble with this, because your deductive approach, and your affinity for seeing the cosmic order of things will be understood and appreciated.

You will need to have enough time and be willing to go round and round in ever smaller circles in order to conclude the deal. If you're used to a linear process, your patience will be severely tested but if you want to be successful, you have no choice but to allow the process to follow its course.

Representation of the sales process for the Marathonians:

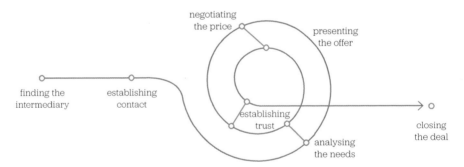

The Marathonians tend not to like talking about the price. It's a subject that's not easily addressed, like with the Diplomats. The subject needs to be approached with care and sensitivity. You might, for example, tell a story about a deal you did at some other time and mention the price obtained in that instance. You might also ask for the price your counterpart paid for a comparable product elsewhere.

AN ANECDOTE FROM A BELGIAN FRIEND:

Jan was sent to China to negotiate the terms of an exhibition of rare objects. His company's offer was received by their Chinese counterpart but the Chinese still wanted to negotiate, so Jan went there for a 24hr return trip. He was given a little bit of flexibility on the price, in order to be able to negotiate and conclude the deal. The meeting was planned for 11am and – important detail – right at the beginning of the meeting, his Chinese counterpart asked Jan when his return flight was. Not suspecting any particular meaning in this question, Jan told him he was flying back very early the next day. Jan found his counterpart's behaviour quite aggressive and by 12:30 Jan had given him his very best offer. The meeting kept on going all afternoon, even though Jan had nothing more to give. By 5pm, he collected all his courage and got ready to leave because it had become obvious to him that they would never reach an agreement. He left his counterpart and went back to the hotel, hopelessly disappointed.

The next morning, Jan checked in at the airport and was waiting for his flight to depart when he was called over the airport public address system and asked to present himself to the information desk. His Chinese counterpart was there with the signed documents and the price that Jan had wanted. He said he had hoped that John would give in at the last moment.

The Chinese can be real players during the negotiation process. You will find that they are willing to take considerable risks to obtain the very best price and every last concession their counterpart may have in their basket of negotiation tools. The Marathonians' low score on uncertainty avoidance (30) is a very good representation of this aspect of their negotiation tactics.

We told the anecdote above to another European businessman experienced in negotiating in China. He smiled and said that he too had learned not to let his counterpart know when he would be flying home.

WHICH ARE THE ARGUMENTS THAT MAKE THE DIFFERENCE?

Once again, the country scores on the Hofstede 6D model will guide us in the choice of our sales arguments. You'll want to make sure you take time to prepare properly and adapt your arguments and the order you present them in to the expectations of your audience. Your presentation can be forceful and engaging just like it would be for the Competitors. Your audience will appreciate the effort you make to convince them, as well as your confidence in yourself and your product or service. Every technique in the book is allowed, from the most modern to the most in-your-face PowerPoint spectacular. If you can, add in a good demonstration of your product or service. The Chinese only want the best.

The Chinese like:
- Personal enhancement
- Formality
- Long-term relationships
- Balanced agreements

Using our example of the wristwatch with a new concept, you will focus on the success of this particular model in Europe, its extraordinary precision due to its permanent satellite connection and the exclusivity that comes with possessing it. However, you'll also stress that this deal represents a unique opportunity for both of your companies as you are both important (or promising) players in this field. On a more personal level, you'll tell your counterpart that it would be a pity if an important person like herself, representing an important company, chose not work with your company, which is widely recognised as a specialist in the field.

The apparent contradiction between the collectivism and masculinity of the Marathonian is a very interesting one. For example, offering your counterpart, a dinner to which he can invite whoever he wants is something totally unheard of in many parts of the world, but is rather effective in China. Don't be surprised that if you say he can invite "whoever he wants", he will take you quite literally and you may find that his invitees have nothing to do with the company. He may invite his family or his friends or whoever else he wants to impress. The point here is that you are providing a means for your counterpart to enhance his personal status in his group, whichever group that is. It is perfectly acceptable to obtain, as part of the bargain, something for you as well, such as some kind of pre-agreement, a declaration of intent, or a factory visit for your engineers. As long as you negotiate patiently and politely, anything is possible.

When you are preparing your arguments, be careful to avoid clichés and stereotypical thinking.

PRESENTATION OF THE PRICE

Contrary to what happens in many other parts of the world, this is not the final step but rather one small step that will need to be repeated over and over. It is not a document that will serve as a future reference. It's just a step in the process. It can be quite simple and straightforward with just the bare minimum of details and it doesn't need to be engaging. Just have a look at how a Chinese car salesman displays the price of his cars. Mostly, you won't even find a price, and when there is one, it will be a 'price of the day', which is subject to change anytime.

PROTECT YOUR KNOWHOW

Make absolutely sure you only provide the absolute minimum of information in your proposal. Simply state the results you will deliver but NOT how you will deliver them. The Chinese come to you because of your knowhow but you MUST shroud it in mystery and not share it. You need to find the right balance between giving enough information to close the deal but not so much that the they understand it all. If they do, they'll end up doing it themselves. Try asking a Chinese chef to give you the recipe for his glazed duck. Have no doubt that he'll send you packing.

THE QUEST FOR BALANCE

The Chinese always keep a bird's-eye view of the entire process. If you find yourself in a situation where you can't or don't want to give in on a specific point, don't hesitate to park it, continue the negotiation process and come back to the specific point at the very end. You might say: "I hope to convince you of our proposal once you've had the opportunity to look at all aspects but this topic is too difficult to finalise right now. Let's move on to the next one."

Remember the difference between compromise and consensus as described in the chapter about the Connected? The Chinese are often looking for a consensus. If you start from a 'black' position, and they start from a 'white' position, the final outcome will often be a new solution which is a mutually acceptable shade of grey, rather than a patchwork of white and black bits, as would be typical for a compromise.

HOW TO ULTIMATELY FINALISE THE DEAL?

This can happen much more suddenly than you might expect and, in an instant, you can become the trusted supplier for this product or that service. You might not even completely understand why the tide suddenly seems to have turned to your advantage.

The day after a meeting or dinner, you'll receive the written order or the signed contract because the moment of equilibrium has been reached, and you may suddenly find that your new client is in a rush to implement the deal.
Several negotiators have told us similar stories. Just when they were giving up hope of reaching a deal, when they were ready to throw in the towel, their counterpart would ask for a couple more hours and would come back with the signed deal.

But it is similarly quite possible that after a day, a month or a year, your Chinese clients will start buying less. This is a signal that he's found another supplier and doesn't want to tell you for risk of insulting you and damaging the relationship.

Yet again, the scores on the Hofstede dimensions will help us understand what is going on. The high score on the masculinity dimension means the Marathonian will want the best possible deal. Therefore, during the negotiation process, make sure you convey the message that he can be proud to have the best, or even the most expensive, product on the market, but that he obtained it at the absolute best price in China or in Asia.

In any case, follow-ups, regular contact and maintenance of the relationship are very important for long-term success. The key issue is that, now that you are the preferred supplier, you need to be aware there will be no signals or alarm bells when someone else is trying to get the business. The only thing you'll see is reduced sales once your competitor is in and by then the damage is done.

RECAP:

- Put in the effort and take the time to choose the right intermediary
- Ask open or multiple-choice questions rather than closed (yes/no) questions
- Be open to a consensus solution rather than a compromise solution
- Never forget the masculine side of the Chinese society
- Keep investing in the relationship and be patient
- Maintain a bird's-eye view of the entire negotiation process
- Only provide a minimum of information and focus on the advantages
- Never forget that there's no need to close the deal during the meeting, let them come to you

NEGOTIATING WITH THE MARATHONIANS

1	Establishing contact	Common friends or intermediaries or very important.
2	Establishing trust	Trust is established on a person to person basis. Acceptance in the circle of trust depends on you personally. During your visit, avoid talking about business but rather spend time to get to know one another.
3	Identifying the needs, presentation of the offer and negoti-ation of the price	Identifying the needs, presentation of the offer (or estimate) and negotiation of the price are all part of one integrated conversation. In the interest of finding common ground or consensus, both parties try to find out what might be of interest for the other party. This may require several rounds. A forceful presentation is appreciated.
4	Closing the deal / re-negotiating the price	The final decision can be taken suddenly and unexpectedly. No alarm bells: invest in maintaining a good relationship.

CHAPTER 12

Mindset 7:

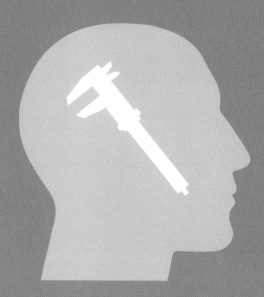

Negotiating with the 'Craftsman'

12

KEY WORDS: precision · reliability · system · process · relationship · timing · fluidity · consensus · honour · save face · indirect communication · continuous improvement

12.1 Why do we call them the Craftsmen?

Because of the attention to detail, the time and effort spent on preparation, the love of elegance, and the passion for perfection that characterises the Craftsman. Even in high volume manufacturing, each object counts, each work station is analysed and optimised, each process is honed, and each improvement executed to achieve the highest possible level of perfection.

So far, we have only encountered this mindset in Japan. The Japanese mindset is very different from any other, but at the same time, somehow combines them all. The Japanese have the elegance of the Diplomats, the passion for order and structure of the Organisers, the proudness and success-orientation of the Competitors, the social connectedness of the Connected and the desire to build long-lasting relationships of the Reciprocators.

It is so special, and the size of the market is so important, that we have dedicated a separate chapter to it. From a Western perspective, we may be tempted to lump the Japanese in with most of South-East Asia, but that would be a mistake. The Japanese are quite different from any other culture. With a strict behavioural etiquette, they have developed a way of living together harmoniously on this densely-populated island.

12.1.1   Unique yet somewhat familiar

You may find the Japanese mindset complex and confusing because anyone who has ever been to Japan for business will recognise familiar aspects of his or her own culture but will also discover others that they find much harder to deal with.

Similar to the Diplomats, the Craftsmen can come across as though they feel somewhat superior to other cultures. In the case of the Diplomats, this is rooted in the belief that they are the heirs of the ancient societies that built the foundations of the Western culture. The Japanese, however, are firmly convinced that they themselves built a superior culture. This belief is experienced by foreign visitors, even if, and probably because, it is wrapped up in a multitude of small, polite gestures and rituals. As mastering these is complex and difficult, it is almost impossible to become part of the in-group. This perpetuates an us-versus-them environment where feelings of superiority thrive. As a result, the Japanese generally prefer to do business with the

Japanese rather than with foreigners, who struggle to understand the uniqueness of Japanese culture.

12.1.2   Hierarchical or not really?

Japan is often thought of as a very hierarchical society. In comparison to many other societies, like the Diplomats, the Reciprocators and the Marathonians, it is actually much less hierarchical. In a truly hierarchical society, the boss decides and the organisation executes. Decisions are always referred to the top of the organisation. This is not the case in Japan. But neither are decisions delegated to the bottom of the organisation, as they are in the Competitor, Connected and Organiser societies.

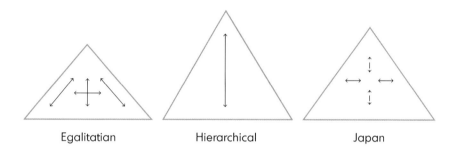

Egalitatian   Hierarchical   Japan

12.1.3   The Nemawashi process

Japan has a unique consensus-finding way of decision-making, which is called Nemawashi. Literally, it means 'digging around the roots' of a tree to prepare it to be moved. In the business context, it should be seen as 'laying the groundwork' and involves a lot of one-on-one conversations with everyone involved. After a while, the solution or the right way to move forward will gently emerge from all these conversations, and the final decision-making is just a formality. It can start at any level in the organisation and builds strength as it moves up towards the top. It is highly unusual for a top manager not to formalise the decision that was prepared for him by the organisation.

12.1.4   Kuuki Yomenai

Another very important skill to be able to negotiate in Japan is KY (of Kuuki Yomenai) which loosely translates as someone's inability to 'read the air'. Communication in Japan is very contextual, very indirect. You always need to watch the body language of other people and place whatever is being said, or not said, in the context within which it was said. For instance, it is considered very impolite to say "no", because it may damage the relationship and/or group harmony. As a consequence, there are a myriad of ways the Japanese will say "yes" but mean varying degrees of "yes but..." or "no". For the hyper-direct, individualist Westerners, being able to 'read the air' and communicate in a less direct way is extremely difficult.

12.1.5   History versus future

The description below of the sales process in Japan is based on its traditional values and ways of functioning. Amongst the younger generation, which is more open to the rest of the world, there seems to be a trend towards Westernisation, and towards doing business in a more 'direct' way. It remains to be seen how much of an impact this will have as we go forward.

RECAP:

- A unique culture
- Quest for perfection
- Relationships first, tasks second
- Nemawashi consensus finding
- Learn how to 'read the air'

	JAPAN	TYPICAL CHARACTERISTICS FOR THE CLUSTER	YOUR SCORE [17]
Power distance	54	Medium	
Individualism	46	Medium	
Masculinity	95	High	
Uncertainty avoidance	92	High	
Long Term Orientation	88	High	
Indulgence vs Restraint	42	Medium	

[17] Please see page 38 on how to determine your own score.

12.2 The 6 steps of the sales process with the Craftsmen

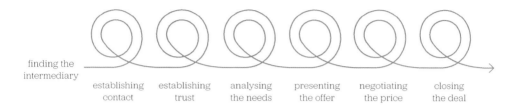

finding the
intermediary

| establishing | establishing | analysing | presenting | negotiating | closing |
| contact | trust | the needs | the offer | the price | the deal |

12.2.1 Establishing contact

As in any other collectivist society, people prefer to do business with people they know and trust. Personal relationships are the lifeblood of business so, as an outsider, your absolute top priority is to create, develop and nurture them. Direct approaches such as cold-calling are a recipe for failure.

As a first step, you need to carefully analyse your own network and see if there is anyone that you trust, who trusts you, who can introduce you to your target customer. If you have someone like that in your network, they are like gold dust. As Japan is a highly-structured society, ideally the person to introduce you should be at the same level or higher than the person you'd like to be introduced to.

If you don't have anyone appropriate in your network, the next best option is to use professional intermediaries such as a Chamber of Commerce or the economic attaché of your embassy. They know the unwritten rules of the game and can be very important allies.

Japanese business people spend a lot of time and energy cultivating their network. According to one of my Japanese friends, any serious businessmen is at most three degrees (three connections) removed from anyone in his industry. Because of this powerful network structure, it is a very good idea to partner with a local company. This gives you access to their entire network and dramatically accelerates your learning curve. At the very minimum, you need to make sure you work with the right intermediaries.

AN ANECDOTE SHARED WITH JEAN-PIERRE BY ONE OF HIS FRIENDS, WHO WE'LL CALL CLAUDE:

Claude's company wanted to find a partner in Japan to develop a highly-promising new activity. The company already had a commercial agency in Tokyo but no experience in this field

in Japan. Claude contacted their agency and suggested he came to Tokyo to start developing contacts. The local Japanese manager dissuaded Claude from coming straight away and asked for time to prepare the visit. "There are only three potential partners," he said. "Please allow us time to find out how best to approach them. We'll do some discreet enquiries about their history, their successes and their failures, and we will find out who the best person to contact is. We need to know their hobbies, their personal situation, the activities of their children..."

Claude acknowledges being somewhat shocked by this approach, as, from his perspective, it wasn't professional. But knowing that their Japanese commercial agency was well respected and highly successful, he went along with it.

Several months later, Claude was invited to Tokyo 'for dinner'. He spent the afternoon with his agent who showed him all the data they had collected on the three potential partners. It was obvious which company should be the preferred partner and luck would have it that Claude's agent was friends with one of the children of a manager at the target company. Through this channel, he had established a friendly rapport of trust and had managed to organise a dinner for Claude and the top manager. Claude was instructed not to talk about business, but rather about his passion for golf in the hope that this might result in an invitation for a game during the following weekend.

Everything had been meticulously anticipated and planned – the dinner, the subjects of conversation, a possible game of golf. If all went well, a conversation about doing business together would ensue, the content of which was also largely prepared already.

12.2.2   Establishing trust

This is the most important and vital step. Personal relationships are the cornerstone of business in Japan. For a large part, trust is built on an interpersonal level and building trust between people takes time. The emotional aspect of the relationship is important. You don't quite need to become friends, but almost. So you need to invest a lot of time in developing relationships and building trust before you can even start to talk about business. It is not unusual to have to make multiple visits and have multiple meetings before one can get down to the topic of business. This can be quite frustrating and feel inefficient for anyone who comes from a more individualistic society, but if you want to do business in Japan, you just have to adapt and be patient.

However, the organisation or the company is a big part of establishing trust. Big is beautiful and a strong brand is a major plus.

In Japan, both aspects of trust are important. If you represent a highly respected, global company, establishing trust will be easier, but it is NOT a free ticket. You still need to dedicate time and effort to developing trust on a personal level as well. If you do not, you are unlikely to be successful and will hurt your own company's reputation in the process.

As in most other collectivist societies, the preservation and development of relationships can be more important than the successful execution of a task. This is because harmony is considered of prime importance for all aspects of life. Looking through the eyes of more individualistic societies, this can take surprisingly extreme forms, where a potential supplier, although he might have an acceptable product or solution, will tell his customer that his solution is not the most appropriate and recommend one of his competitors who has a better solution. In the short term, he loses out, but by recommending his competitor, he strengthens the relationship, which, in the long run, will be beneficial for him.

Another important element of building trust is 'nomunication' which stems from the Japanese word 'nomu' (to drink) and 'communication'. Drinking together after work is an essential part of Japanese corporate life. During the day, work life is highly structured and regulated with a lot of norms to adhere to. However, in order to really get to know someone, it is essential guards are let down, inhibitions overcome and one's true self is shown. This is the purpose of nomunication. Drinking until 'one falls over' is a way to get rid of all barriers and really connect with a person. It shows that you are willing to show your true self. Westerners often worry about making a fool of themselves and feel it is unprofessional behaviour. But they have missed the point, because this experience is all about developing the relationship and building trust. Just like 'whatever happens in Vegas, stays in Vegas,' whatever happens during nomunication, stays there and is never ever mentioned in the office. So if you are trying to develop commercial relationships in Japan, be ready to take part in and/or invite your customer for a nomunication evening. If you can't drink for medical or other reasons, there are alternatives such as karaoke bars where you can still let your guard down without having to get drunk.

12.2.3   Identifying the needs

In this step, several particularities of Japanese society are important:
- You need to be aware of the Nemawashi process and play by its rules.
- There are two dimensions to hierarchy. One is the organisational hierarchy and the other is seniority and experience. The combination of these will define who you need to develop a relationship with and how to do it.

	GROUP A Keep informed, entice them with technical superiority of your product/solution	GROUP B Build a very strong relationship / wine and dine / play golf, etc.
SENIORITY AND EXPERIENCE ↑	GROUP C Keep informed	GROUP D Build a very strong relationship / wine and dine / play golf etc.

ORGANISATIONAL HIERARCHY →

In order to find out what the needs of the organisation are, you need to identify who in groups B and D you need to talk to and build a relationship with. You can then begin to ask questions about what their problems are, how you might be able to help them, etc. You need to have these conversations with as many people as possible and generally approach the subject in an indirect way. After a while, the needs of your customer, as well as acceptable commercial conditions, will 'emerge' from this Nemawashi approach.

Make sure all your documentation, including your company presentation, are of high quality.

12.2.4   Presenting the proposal

The purpose of your formal proposal is to confirm all the details, which have been discussed between both parties. The document needs to be very clear, very detailed and well presented. It is much more than just a confirmation of price. We recommend you make the effort to hand the proposal to your customer in a personal meeting. Never miss an opportunity to strengthen the relationship.

12.2.5   Negotiating the price

If you have handled the Nemawashi process well, the price will have been part of your many conversations. Price discussions are delicate. Like the Diplomats, the Craftsmen are reluctant to talk about money and feel it may damage harmony or cause them to lose face. Nevertheless, business is business and the conversation must be had. As a supplier, you present your offer considering your costs and your margin. Your customer may ask for a reduction and will typically justify his request with arguments related to his current supplier, a competitor's offer or market prices. It is quite possible he will tell you, or perhaps have already told you, the price he wants.

If a different price is requested, you should take that information and request some time to reflect and consult your organisation before responding. Even if you have the authority or mandate from your organisation to make the necessary decisions to close the deal right there and then, don't be tempted to do so. We recommend you pretend you need to consult your organisation.

In Japan, making the best possible decision for the long term is FAR more important than making a decision quickly. As a consequence, having to go through several rounds of consultation with the respective organisations is quite normal. Keep in mind that you are most likely negotiating with someone who does not have a mandate from his organisation to make final decisions. He needs time to work the internal Nemawashi process, to make sure all stakeholders are aligned, until, slowly but surely, it becomes obvious to all concerned that working with you is in the best long-term interests of the whole organisation. Short-term gains and quick wins, so common in many parts of the Western world, are generally not of interest.

Never forget KY (Kuuki Yomenai). Always keep the need to read the air in your mind, to avoid misreading the messages your customer is sending you.

Remember that although Japan seems very hierarchical, compared to many other societies it really isn't. Decisions are not made at the top – they are made by the collective of the organisation through the Nemawashi process and then presented to the top for formal validation. The core of a Japanese CEO's job is to formally validate whatever decision the collective has come up with. She herself will probably have taken part in the Nemawashi process, so will be fully aware of all aspects of the decision.

NEGOTIATION TRAINING

Normally, a serious company has a price list and should stick to it. Of course, rebates can apply for especially large accounts etc. Be aware that many buyers are trained to ask at least three times for a bigger rebate. Make sure that you have also done some training on how to say no in a socially acceptable manner.

12.2.6 Closing the deal

Typically, the final step is a meeting with the top manager to confirm the deal. It is of strategic importance, in terms of building a deeper and long-lasting relationship, to have a meeting with top management when closing the deal. It shows your respect for the top management by visiting and formally acquiring approval directly from them. Because the Nemawashi process makes most people part of the decision, the top management doesn't have the opportunity to show their authority except in this meeting. It is far better to have a meeting than to make a phone call or just write an email when closing the deal. The meeting is kind of a ceremony for the top management to show its authority.

Keep in mind that, like the Connected, the Craftsman may have a very strong relationship with his current supplier. It may be the case that your offer will be shown to the current supplier and that she will be offered an opportunity to align her conditions and services to keep the business. However, this would normally happen during the Nemawashi process, not at the very end when closing the deal.

After closing the deal, keep investing in the relationship, to develop and intensify it further. Organise follow-up meetings and don't forget to arrange dinner and drinks parties (nomunication), as these will be the times when you will have the opportunity to get real insight into how the relationship is developing, and how happy they are with your products or services.

SOME MORE ADVICE
A well-kept secret (at least for the outside world) is that all the actors in a certain industry or trade know each other very well. Even direct competitors have good relationships which manifests itself in a kind of natural sharing of the market. As all players have their strengths and weaknesses, they guide one-another to each other. Since everyone is looking for the best long-term solution to their need, the market finds these natural and mostly harmonious partnerships.

Therefore, it is really hard to break into a market from outside Japan. It is much better to establish local partnerships, work with local middlemen and let them do the legwork, working the Nemawashi process until the decision has been prepared. That is the time when you, as the high-level representative of your company, will meet an equally high-level representative of your customer's company and formally close the deal. Each and every aspect of the deal will have been fine-tuned earlier so there is no risk of losing face.

RECAP:

- Kuuki Yomenai (KY): learn how to read the air
- Nemawashi (digging around the roots): the process of development of consensus
- Nomunication: this is when you will discover the real needs and/or issues
- The Japanese society is very masculine so ultimate success is really important
- The Japanese society is extremely uncertainty avoidant
- Keep investing in the relationship, spend time together, wine and dine, and do karaoke together

NEGOTIATING WITH THE CRAFTSMEN

1	Establishing contact	Build on existing relationships in your network or use intermediaries.
2	Establishing trust	This takes a long time. Nomunication!
3	Identifying the needs	Identify the experts and the people with seniority. Beware of the Nemawashi process.
4	Presenting the commercial proposal	Clear and detailed recap of the outcome of the Nemawashi conversations.
5	Negotiating the price	Kuuki Yomenai. Learn how to read the air and how to say no in an appropriate way.
6	Closing the deal	This is simply a formalisation of the outcome of the Nemawashi process.

CHAPTER 13

The Science of Culture

13

Our approach in this book is based on four key elements:
- · The scientific work of Prof. Emeritus Geert Hofstede which resulted in his 6D model of national cultures
- · The clustering of countries by Huib Wursten into seven groups of countries that, at a helicopter level, function in a similar fashion.
- · Our model of the B2B sales process
- · Our own experience as well as contributions from countless other professionals

We have built our system on the backbone of Hofstede's 6D model and, in this chapter, we attempt to provide you with a bird's-eye view and summary of his work. We highly recommend you read his latest book: *Cultures and Organisations: Software of the Mind* [18].

ABOUT GEERT HOFSTEDE AND THE HISTORY OF THE 6D MODEL
(a selection from Wikipedia [19] and www.hofstede-insights.com)

Geert Hofstede first graduated as a mechanical engineer from the University of Delft (Netherlands). After working in industry for ten years, he started studying social psychology. He obtained his PhD from the University of Groningen (Netherlands) and is Professor Emeritus of Organisational Anthropology and International Management at Maastricht University in the Netherlands.

In 1965, he joined IBM International, working as a management trainer and manager of personnel research. He founded and managed the Personnel Research Department. This was his transition from the field of engineering and into psychology. In this role, he played an active part in the introduction and application of employee opinion surveys in over 70 national subsidiaries of IBM around the world. He travelled across Europe and the Middle East to interview people and conduct surveys regarding people's behaviour in large organisations and how they collaborated. At the time, the results of the IBM's surveys, with more than 110,000 completed questionnaires, were one of the largest cross-national databases that existed. Between 1973 and 1979, he worked on the data, and analysed it in a variety of ways. He used existing literature in psychology, sociology, political science and anthropology to relate his findings to a larger scope of study. The data covered more than 70 countries, from which Hofstede first used the 40 countries with the largest groups of respondents, and afterwards extended the analysis to 50 countries and three regions. Subsequent studies validating the earlier results include such respondent groups as

18 Cultures and Organizations, Software of the Mind. Intercultural Cooperation and its importance for survival by Geert Hofstede, Gert Jan Hofstede and Michael Minkov, published by McGraw Hill 2010

19 Source: Wikipedia https://en.wikipedia.org/wiki/Geert_Hofstede

commercial airline pilots and students in 23 countries, civil service managers in 14 counties, 'up-market' consumers in 15 countries and 'elites' in 19 countries.

The values that distinguished country cultures from each other could be statistically categorised into four groups. These four groups became the Hofstede dimensions of national culture:

- Power Distance (PDI)
- Individualism versus Collectivism (IDV)
- Masculinity versus Femininity (MAS)
- Uncertainty Avoidance (UAI)

A fifth dimension was added in 1991 based on research by Michael Harris Bond, supported by Hofstede. Bond conducted an additional international study among students with a survey instrument that was developed together with Chinese professors. That dimension, based on Confucian thinking, was called Long Term Orientation (LTO) and was applied to 23 countries.

In 2010, research by Michael Minkov generated two dimensions using recent World Values Survey data from representative samples of national populations. One was a new dimension, and the second was more or less a replication of the fifth dimension. The number of country scores for the fifth dimension could now be extended to 93.

In the 2010 edition of Cultures and Organisations, a sixth dimension has been added, based on Michael Minkov's analysis of the World Values Survey data for 93 countries. This new dimension is called Indulgence versus Restraint (IND).

Hofstede received many honorary awards, and in 2011 was made a Knight of the Order of the Netherlands Lion (Orde van de Nederlandse Leeuw). He holds honorary doctorates from seven universities in Europe, (Nyenrode Business University, New Bulgarian University, Athens University of Economics and Business, University of Gothenburg, University of Liège, ISM University of Management and Economics, University of Pécs in 2009, and University of Tartu in 2012). He also received honorary professorships at The University of Hong Kong (1992–2000), the Beijing University of International Business and Economics (UIBE), and the Renmin University of China in Beijing.

PROF. GEERT HOFSTEDE'S DEFINITION OF CULTURE

Hofstede has defined culture as "the collective programming of the mind that distinguishes the members of one group or category of people from others".

THE DIFFERENT LEVELS OF CULTURE

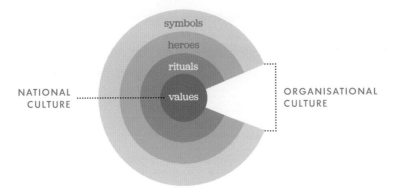

The culture of a group of people or societies is expressed in various ways. Hofstede developed the 'onion' model represented in the image above. As you go from the outside layer inwards, you reach the core, which represents the fundamental values of the society. These are hard to see and most members of a society aren't even consciously aware of them. However, they are the core foundation on which everything else is built and, therefore, understanding and visualising them is a powerful tool in any intercultural setting. National culture is about the value differences between groups of nations and/or regions.

GLOBALISATION AND CULTURE

The ever accelerating globalisation and internationalisation of our world, driven by social media tools like Facebook, Instagram, or WhatsApp, may lead one to think that cultures must be rapidly converging. There is some convergence of the outer layers of culture but, so far, there is no data to show that there is a convergence of the core values. One of the explanations for this may be that humans acquire their core values very early on in life. They are bestowed on us by our parents and our immediate environment, which tell us what is 'right' and 'wrong', and how to behave 'properly'. Social sciences teach us that this programming is largely complete by the time we are ten to twelve years old, and that it hardly changes regardless of our experiences later on in life. As adults, we then bestow these same (or, at most, slightly altered) values on our children. The result is that cultural change happens really slowly.

In the past, as a rule of thumb, when people moved away from their homes to other countries, the first generation born in the new home country would partly integrate and have a hybrid culture. Generally, only their children would be fully integrated and have absorbed the culture of the country.

Contrary to the popular belief that social medial is a good tool for integration, it is also a tool for maintaining connection with the home country. This means that preserving one's original cultural programming, rather than adopting the host country's culture, has become much easier. Only time will tell which way the pendulum will swing.

13.1 The 6D model explained

The model of national culture consists of six dimensions. These cultural dimensions represent statistically independent preferences for one state of affairs over another that distinguish countries (rather than individuals) from each other. The country scores in each of the dimensions are relative, as we are all human and we are all unique. In other words, culture can be only used meaningfully by comparison.

It is important to understand that the country values on the six cultural dimensions are average values for a country or region. By no means do they imply that the behaviour of every person in that country can be understood by looking at these values. The score is just the average value of a large sample of people and within the sample there is substantial variation. This is best graphically represented by using a bell curve or Gaussian distribution where the peak of the curve represents the average value or country score, but we will also find any other value along the curve.

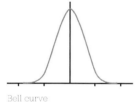

Bell curve

Different scores for two countries are best represented by overlapping curves. The peaks are different but there is an overlap between the curves meaning that, on average, the behaviour is different. However, the blue area represents people in each respective country that exhibit similar behaviour. The further apart the scores or the further away the peaks of the curve, the more different the culture will be and the less likely it will be that there is an overlap.

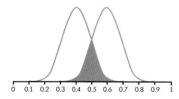

0   0.1   0.2   0.3   0.4   0.5   0.6   0.7   0.8   0.9   1

Overlapping Bell curves

Hofstede's research shows that, in order to be statistically significant and noticeable in daily life, the difference in scores between two countries needs to be at least ten.

13.1.1　Power Distance Index (PDI) or attitude towards hierarchy

This dimension expresses the degree to which the less powerful members of a society accept and expect that power is distributed unequally. The fundamental issue here is how a society handles inequalities among people.

People in societies exhibiting a large degree of Power Distance accept a hierarchical order in which everybody has a place and no further justification is needed. Status is not achieved but ascribed. Status is expected to be shown and age is respected. In societies with low Power Distance scores, people strive to equalise the distribution of power and demand justification for inequalities of power. People with power and status will strive to minimise status symbols and try hard to be 'just one of the girls or boys'.

This dimension has major implications for the way a country or organisation is structured and organised. In societies that have a low score on this dimension, one can say that hierarchy is there for convenience. It is not about power, delegation is natural, and people lower down in an organisation expect to be consulted, to take responsibility and to make decisions. The ideal leader is a facilitator who consults and coordinates.

On the opposite side of the spectrum, hierarchy is an expression of existential inequalities that are just part of life. Decision making is centralised and the rest of the organisation is expected to execute and not question. It is considered normal that the higher up in the organisation one is, the more special privileges one has. The ideal leader is autocratic.

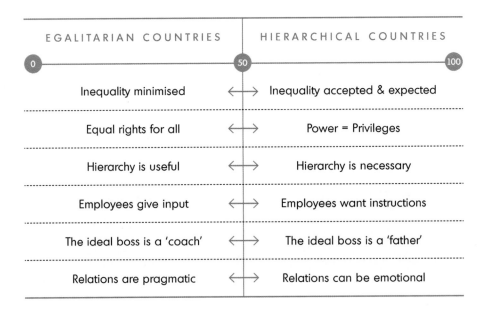

EGALITARIAN COUNTRIES		HIERARCHICAL COUNTRIES
0	50	100
Inequality minimised	←→	Inequality accepted & expected
Equal rights for all	←→	Power = Privileges
Hierarchy is useful	←→	Hierarchy is necessary
Employees give input	←→	Employees want instructions
The ideal boss is a 'coach'	←→	The ideal boss is a 'father'
Relations are pragmatic	←→	Relations can be emotional

13.1.2   Individualism versus Collectivism (IDV) or attitude towards groups

The higher side of this dimension, called individualism, can be defined as a preference for a loosely-knit social framework, in which individuals are only expected to take care of themselves and their immediate families. Its opposite, collectivism, represents a preference for a tightly-knit social framework, in which individuals can expect their relatives or members of a particular in-group to look after them in exchange for unquestioning loyalty.

A society's score on this dimension is reflected in whether people's self-image is defined in terms of 'I' or 'we'. Communication tends to be more explicit and verbal in individualist countries, whereas in collectivist countries, reading between the lines (implicit or 'high context' communication) is the norm. In individualist societies, people tend to prioritise the successful execution of a task or a contract over developing and maintaining relationships. On the opposite end, in collectivist societies, developing and maintaining relationships comes first and the successful execution of tasks comes second.

When an individual makes a mistake in an individualistic society, she will feel guilt and her self-esteem will be hurt. In collectivist societies, that individual will more likely feel shame because she let her group down.

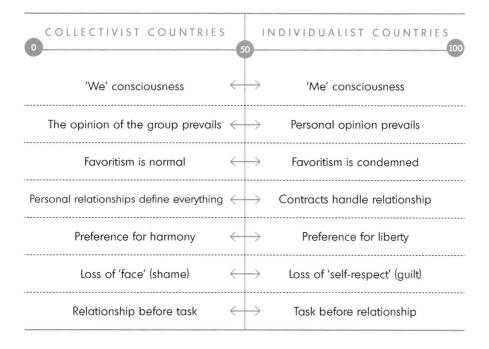

COLLECTIVIST COUNTRIES		INDIVIDUALIST COUNTRIES
0	50	100
'We' consciousness	←→	'Me' consciousness
The opinion of the group prevails	←→	Personal opinion prevails
Favoritism is normal	←→	Favoritism is condemned
Personal relationships define everything	←→	Contracts handle relationship
Preference for harmony	←→	Preference for liberty
Loss of 'face' (shame)	←→	Loss of 'self-respect' (guilt)
Relationship before task	←→	Task before relationship

13.1.3 Masculinity versus Femininity (MAS) or attitude towards motivation[20]

Masculinity stands for a society in which social gender roles are clearly distinct: Men are supposed to be assertive, tough, and focused on material success. Women are supposed to be more modest, tender, and concerned with the quality of life. Society at large is more competitive. Status is obtained through success. In these societies, although it is more and more acceptable for women to be assertive, tough and focused on material success, it is generally NOT acceptable for men to be modest, tender and concerned with quality of life. Japan is a good example of such a country.

Femininity stands for a society in which social gender roles overlap substantially. Both men and women are supposed to be modest, tender and concerned with the quality of life. These societies will tend to have strong social support networks, generous parental leave provisions for both parents, strong social security systems, and a work to live ethic. Very good examples are found in the Nordic countries.

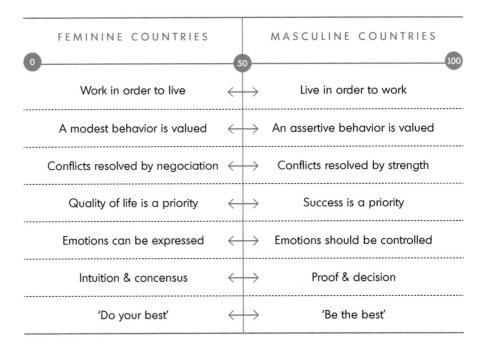

FEMININE COUNTRIES		MASCULINE COUNTRIES
0	50	100
Work in order to live	⟷	Live in order to work
A modest behavior is valued	⟷	An assertive behavior is valued
Conflicts resolved by negociation	⟷	Conflicts resolved by strength
Quality of life is a priority	⟷	Success is a priority
Emotions can be expressed	⟷	Emotions should be controlled
Intuition & concensus	⟷	Proof & decision
'Do your best'	⟷	'Be the best'

20 As mentioned earlier, the description Masculinity versus Femininity can be a source of controversy, especially in societies that score relatively highly on this scale. We decided to keep Hofstede's original description as we are not qualified to change this very common and well-understood terminology in the social sciences.
We would like to suggest to the reader that they can think of this dimension as 'Tough' versus 'Soft'.
For further information, we refer to www.hofstede insights.com.

13.1.4 Uncertainty Avoidance Index (UAI) or attitude towards uncertainty

The uncertainty avoidance dimension expresses the degree to which the members of a society feel uncomfortable with uncertainty and ambiguity. The fundamental issue here is how a society deals with the fact that the future can never be known – should we try to control the future or just let it happen? Countries exhibiting high uncertainty avoidance scores maintain rigid codes of belief and behaviour, and are intolerant of unorthodox behaviour and ideas. There is a need for rules and formality to structure life. Competence and expertise are highly valued. Societies with low uncertainty avoidance scores maintain a more relaxed attitude, in which practice counts more than principles. People tend to be more entrepreneurial and innovative.

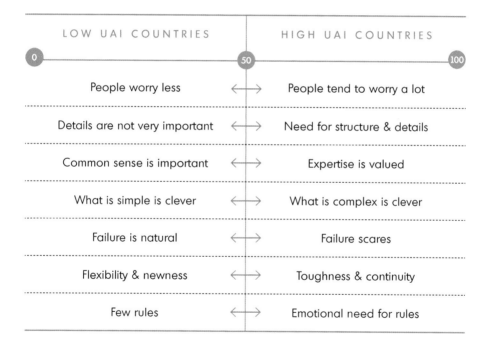

LOW UAI COUNTRIES		HIGH UAI COUNTRIES
0	50	100
People worry less	←→	People tend to worry a lot
Details are not very important	←→	Need for structure & details
Common sense is important	←→	Expertise is valued
What is simple is clever	←→	What is complex is clever
Failure is natural	←→	Failure scares
Flexibility & newness	←→	Toughness & continuity
Few rules	←→	Emotional need for rules

13.1.5   Long Term Orientation (LTO) or attitude towards time

Every society has to maintain some links with its own past while dealing with the challenges of the present and the future. Societies prioritise these two existential goals differently.

Societies who have a low score on this dimension prefer to maintain time-honoured traditions and norms, while viewing societal change with suspicion. Those with a culture which scores highly, on the other hand, take a more pragmatic approach – they encourage thrift and efforts in modern education as a way to prepare for the future.

     In a business context, this dimension is referred to as (short term) normative versus (long term) pragmatic.

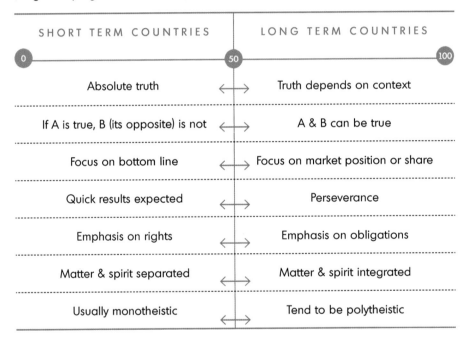

SHORT TERM COUNTRIES		LONG TERM COUNTRIES
0	50	100
Absolute truth	←→	Truth depends on context
If A is true, B (its opposite) is not	←→	A & B can be true
Focus on bottom line	←→	Focus on market position or share
Quick results expected	←→	Perseverance
Emphasis on rights	←→	Emphasis on obligations
Matter & spirit separated	←→	Matter & spirit integrated
Usually monotheistic	←→	Tend to be polytheistic

13.1.6 Indulgence versus Restraint (IND) or attitude towards happiness

A high indulgence score stands for a society that allows relatively free gratification of basic and natural human drives related to enjoying life and having fun. A lower score, on the restraint end of the spectrum, stands for a society that suppresses the gratification of needs and regulates it by means of strict social norms.

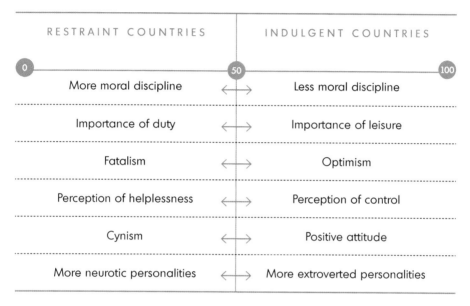

RESTRAINT COUNTRIES		INDULGENT COUNTRIES
More moral discipline	←→	Less moral discipline
Importance of duty	←→	Importance of leisure
Fatalism	←→	Optimism
Perception of helplessness	←→	Perception of control
Cynism	←→	Positive attitude
More neurotic personalities	←→	More extroverted personalities

13.1.7   Huib Wursten's Culture Clusters[©][21]

In his work with complex international organisations, Wursten realised that understanding the Hofstede dimensions individually was not enough to explain the complexity of real life issues. In discussions, he found himself mostly explaining and analysing the situation by combining two, three or all of dimensions. He concluded this was more effective than looking at the dimensions one by one. It was also simpler, and easier to capture, remember and apply. This led him to develop the 6 Culture Clusters[©] with associated Mental Images[©].

CONTEST	NETWORK	MACHINE	SOLAR SYSTEM	PYRAMID	FAMILY
PDI IDV MAS UAI	PDI IDV MAS UAI	PDI IDV MAS UAI	PDI IDV MAS UAI	PDI IDV MAS UAI	PDI IDV MAS UAI
↘ ↗ ↗ ↘	↘ ↗ ↗ →	↘ ↗ ↗ ↗	↗ ↗ → ↗	↗ ↘ → ↗	↗ ↘ → ↘
USA	Sweden	Germany	France	Guatemala	Singapore
UK	Netherlands	Switzerland (G.)	Belgium	Brazil	Hong Kong
Ireland	Norway	Czech rep.	Switzerland (Fr.)	Russia	China
New Zealand	Finland	Hungary	Italy (N.)	Turkey	Thailand
Australia	Denmark	Austria	Poland	Portugal	India
Canada	Baltics	Luxembourg	Spain	S. Korea	Malaysia
Competition	Consensus	Structure	Hierarchy	Hierarchy	Hierarchy
Autonomy	Cooperation	Autonomy	Rules	Loyalty	Loyalty
Decentralisation	Decentralisation	Decentralisation	Centralisation	Centralisation	Centralisation
Risk-taking	Risk-taking	Procedures	Formality	Formality	Harmony
Results	Well being	Calculated risk	Analyses	Procedures	Flexibility
Ambition	Reliability	Expertise	Honour	Respect	Indirect
Innovation	Social ethics	Expert needs	Well being	Indirect Communication	Communication

21 Extracts from a paper written by Huib Wursten 'Mental images of culture, a perspective to understand misunderstandings in politics, business, religion & ... to make some sense of the challenges in today's confusing world, available by sending a request to the author by email to huib.wursten@hofstede-insights.com.

For the purpose of our book we have chosen different mental images that are more appropriate for the typical negotiation behaviour of each cluster.

- Contest = The Competitor
- Network = The Connected
- Machine = The Organiser
- Solar = The Diplomat
- Pyramid = The Reciprocator
- Family = The Marathonian

JAPAN

As discussed in Chapter 12, Japan is quite special and doesn't fit into any of the above clusters, so from a national cultural perspective, it stands by itself. We called them 'The Craftsmen'.

PDI IDV MAS UAI

→ → ⁄ ⁄

Structure

Perfection

Harmony

Consensus

Honour

Formality

Indirect

Communication

13.2 Deductive versus Inductive reasoning

Writing a book on negotiation and making it salient and useful for as large an audience as possible is a challenge. If you consider that there is a strong cultural aspect in everyone's approach to learning and problem solving, it becomes even more difficult. Broadly speaking, the way we approach solving problems and hence the way we are used to being taught, can be divided in two distinct mindsets: deductive or inductive.

If you're from a culture that functions in a deductive way, you will have learned to solve problems by taking a step back to try and get a bird's-eye view of the situation, to understand the bigger picture and the overall theory, so that you can then figure out what the source of the problem is, and what is creating a kind of disharmony in the whole. Only then will you make decisions and take steps to sort out the specific source of the problem. Your key driver is to try and truly understand the why and the how of the whole situation. A deductive culture deduces the solution from theory, observations and analysis. A lot of European countries tend to function in a deductive way.

If you're from an inductive culture, you'll prefer to quickly try a solution that shows a decent likelihood of success, and if it doesn't work, try another and another until you find the one that works. An inductive culture induces the solution from a series of carefully considered experiments. Approaches like trial and error, 'try quickly, fail quickly, change quickly' and the use of best practices are typical for inductive cultures. People in these cultures are far less concerned with understanding why a solution works than in deductive cultures. They'll simply try something and if it works, that is good enough and it can be translated into best practice. Anglo-Saxons tend to function like this. Harvard Business School is well known for its case-based approach to teaching and learning. Students study a series of real-life business cases and draw conclusions about what works and what doesn't. The focus is more on establishing best practice rather than on the question of why things worked or didn't work.

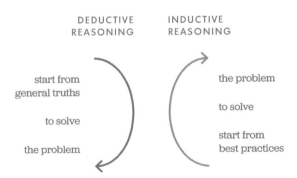

DEDUCTIVE REASONING

INDUCTIVE REASONING

start from general truths

to solve

the problem

the problem

to solve

start from best practices

AN EXAMPLE TO PAINT A CLEAR (ALBEIT EXAGGERATED) PICTURE:

Someone from a deductive culture may start a presentation on the quality of his safety equipment for an application in the marine industry as follows: "We all know there is a cosmic order, the planets follow their well-known trajectories, the tides are a consequence of lunar attraction, we're selling safety material for ships and our warranty systems is so advanced that it takes the effect of tidal exposure of the silicone seals into account."

The deductive person finds this type of reasoning reassuring and intelligent at the same time. It places the topic right in the centre of the bigger general truths of the entire cosmos. Good examples of cultures who love this approach are the French and the Russians.

Inductive reasoning doesn't work like that at all. It starts from the opposite end. The inductive customer (perhaps a Brit, Australian or American) might ask: "I have a problem with wear on the silicon joints because of marine salt exposure. Who can help me solve this problem quickly and efficiently?"

If you try to sell your solution to her by building your sales arguments on deductive reasoning, she'll very quickly start to yawn from sheer boredom, while thinking "When is he going to get to the point?"

So, forget the deductive build-up all together and simply present your arguments along the lines of: "You called me to help solve your problems of premature wear of the silicone seals. We have a large range of products that are highly successful in the sector of application X and Y, which are very similar to your problem. I'm absolutely confident that we can solve your problem as well."

Inversely, if you are trying to sell your solution to someone from a deductive culture, be prepared to substantiate your arguments far beyond best practices and practical proof. The deductive customer will want to understand why your solution is the best, and what the underlying theory and/or the academic foundation is.

13

13.3 Key differences in negotiation styles between individualist and collectivist societies

When looking at Wursten's culture clusters, four clusters share a common characteristic, which is a high to very high score in individualism. We are sure it is obvious to you that negotiating with a culture that emphasises the 'I' is very different from negotiating with a culture that emphasises the 'we'. The individualist clusters tend to be task oriented and collectivist countries tend to be more relationship oriented. Each individualist cluster has a different way of accomplishing whatever the task at hand is, and each places a different value on relationships, but for all of them, successful accomplishment of the task comes first.

These four individualist clusters cover most of the economically successful Western world. This is very interesting and may lead us to the conclusion that a focus on the individual (high IDV) is the one and only right formula for success as defined by financial wealth. Research has shown that indeed there seems to be a correlation between the wealth of a nation as measured by GDP per capita and individualism. Over time, the wealthier a nation becomes, the more the score on individualism seems to increase. However, it doesn't seem to be that we're more successful because we're more individualist, but rather that we are becoming more individualist as we become wealthier. Just look at the Asian tiger economies and you'll start to see what we mean.

'WE' VERSUS 'I'
First, we need to clarify how the collectivist societies see 'we', as it is very different from the way 'we' is perceived in individualist societies. If, like us, you are from an individualistic society, it is very likely your understanding of a group is of it as a collection of individuals that are somehow linked together to form a group.

A simple example to illustrate: If we were to address a group and say "Let's go for lunch", we wouldn't really be addressing the group as a collective, but rather each individual collectively. We would expect individual responses which could be anything from "I can't yet" to "Let's go, I'm hungry", depending on how each individual feels. We would not expect a group reply.

However, collectivists see it completely differently. As a matter of fact, one might consider it to be a mirror image of how individualists see the 'we'. Let us use the expression 'the collective', as it best describes the 'we' as seen by collectivists. The collective is a unique and very strong entity that is accountable for all. The individual is just one part of the collective – an organ in a body, so to speak, and not really a unit or an identity in itself.

For the individualist, the collective is an invisible, elusive entity that can be really hard to understand. But for the collectivist, the collective provides everything an individual needs: comfort and protection, but also stimulus, creativity and challenge. The individual lives his entire life within the safety and security of the cocoon that is the collective. He learns how to be useful to the group and serve it in his role as father, worker, husband, boss, etc. He derives fulfilment from the knowledge that his life has purpose as one piece of a bigger collective.

The images below illustrate the difference in perception of the 'we' between individualists and collectivists.

'WE' AS SEEN BY THE INDIVIDUALISTS | 'WE' AS SEEN BY THE COLLECTIVISTS

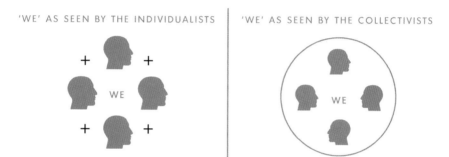

In a collectivist society, the interests of the individual are subordinate to those of the group. In return the group provides protection and support for the individual. Unlike the individualist societies, collectivist societies are very much relationship oriented rather than task oriented.

A PERSONAL ANECDOTE (WHICH WE HAVE DISCUSSED FROM A DIFFERENT PERSPECTIVE BEFORE):

Jean-Pierre was planning to visit his son who lives and works in China and wanted the use the opportunity to gain some experience by spending a day or two prospecting for new clients. So he asked his son for the contact information of a handful of major companies and, if possible, the name of the HR manager, hoping he would end up with two or three prospects. Jean-Pierre was very surprised when the next day, he received a list of 500 companies which a friend, working in the interim labour industry, had secured for him. Enthusiastically, he contacted all the well-known ones and unsurprisingly (in hindsight), he never heard back from any of them. In the end, he managed to secure three meetings, all of which were arranged through intermediaries in the form of his personal relations or the Chamber of Commerce.

An important lesson is that cold-calling, as you may know it in individualistic societies, simply doesn't work. Trying to do this is considered inappropriate or even indecent. In China as well as in Japan, one doesn't do business with strangers. One does business with friends or friends of friends or someone who knows someone who knows a friend. For someone from an individualist country, getting your mind around this can be a real challenge and require continuous effort. It may even feel wrong to you to develop business like this, as it may clash with your values.

People from many individualist countries pride themselves on the strict separation between their business activities and their personal life. They tend to feel strongly that it is ethically correct to do so and may even think that this gives them the moral high ground. Most people in the world live in collectivist societies and don't see it that way at all. They find it hard to see how you could possibly build trust in a business relationship if you don't know one another personally, or at least, if you weren't recommended by a trusted friend. There is also a geographic and historic link with the rule of law. Think of it like this: If you live in a society where the rule of law is respected by everyone, you can trust that your counterpart will also follow the same laws you do, and hence trust is built on the basis that you are sure you will both follow the same rules and regulations. You don't need the personal relationship to add value to the transaction or to reduce business risk and therefore you can allow yourself to be task-focused. In parts of the world where you don't have the strong rule of law or cannot trust it, this poses an existential personal and business risk. What can you to do mitigate this risk? The answer now seems obvious. You can decide to live, play, work and do business only with people you know and trust. The group you belong to and the people you trust are of existential importance. Why would you risk doing business with people you don't know if you don't have a legal framework and the power of the rule of law to solve conflicts that may arise? Maintaining the integrity of the group, and continuously strengthening the circle of trust, is always, logically, the top priority in anything an individual does. In this way, the interest of the individual is aligned with the interest of the group, and there is quite a harmonious relationship between the 'we' and the 'I'.

Personal relationships are the single most important factor in doing business with the Collectivists. That said, is it hard to transfer your relationship to a successor? Not really if done appropriately. You need to introduce your successor personally to each of your relations and make sure enough time is spent to assure a proper transfer of the relationship. Plan a sufficiently long transition period so you are still there while the relationship slowly transfers to your successor. This way, the passing of the baton is properly executed and the business will remain securely anchored. If you don't do this properly, your business is at risk and your successor will have to start from square one.

FAVORITISM AND LOYALTY

Favoritism (or Nepotism) is an evil word for anyone from an individualist society. However, in collectivist societies it is seen differently. The individualist mindset is programmed to think favoritism is unacceptable and sees it as the individual who abuses his or her power to the benefit of family and friends. We need to clearly distinguish between favoritism and corruption. The latter is never acceptable, anywhere, anytime. But let's face it, especially in family companies, favoritism is omnipresent and accepted in the individualist world as well. How it manifests itself is very dependent on the cultural context.

For the collectivists, a leader is a part of the collective who is able to help the group. Nobody in his group would understand it if he refused something (e.g. to appoint people from his collective) that would benefit the group as a whole. From an individualistic perspective, this may still be hard to chew on but at least you should recognise that the situation is quite different and needs to be seen within its cultural context. Obviously, clear abuse of power and profiteering from it is unacceptable regardless of the cultural context, but the lesson is to observe and understand first before judging according to one's own moral and ethical framework.

DIRECT VERSUS INDIRECT COMMUNICATION

Generally, etiquette in collectivist countries does not allow you to answer a question with "no". You may think that a clear no can be very helpful but in the eyes of people from collectivist societies, it is extremely impolite and offensive. You will find that collectivists never answer a question with no but rather have a whole range of variations of yes, yes-maybe, and possibly.

If you are from an individualist society, you want to make a habit of asking open-ended questions that cannot be answered with a simple "yes" or "no", or use a multiple-choice approach such as: "If I offer you option A, will you consider me as primary or as secondary supplier?" This will give your customer the opportunity to answer "secondary supplier" without having to be impolite or afraid of insulting you. This way, she lets you know politely that your offer isn't top notch and gives you an opportunity to improve it. If you would have asked if your proposal met her needs, you would most likely have found yourself in a position where she wouldn't have said "no" because that is considered impolite and misunderstandings would have started to accumulate.

Another option you have is to answer a question with a question.

13.4 Relationship with time

Hofstede's fifth dimension, Long Term Orientation, is of particular importance in many Far Eastern collectivist societies. In general, the Asian countries have higher scores. The Middle East and Latin-American countries tend to score on the middle to low range, whereas Northern-African countries tend to be on the very low end.

A high score in this dimension means that:
- There are no absolute truths. You will often find many religions and/or belief systems co-existing peacefully (e.g. Shintoism & Buddhism in Japan).
- Change is accepted easily.
- Perseverance is expected.
- The approach will be pragmatic, which means that principles are not absolute and to be seen within a context.
- Long-term success is more important than short-term gain.

A low score on this dimension means that:
- People tend to think in absolute truths. Something is either 'right' or 'wrong'.
- Short-term gain is the priority.

Although this dimension has an influence on international negotiation, for the purpose of this book, we have chosen not to subdivide Wursten's Pyramid Cluster along this dimension. We have opted to maintain a helicopter view and our general guidelines from the section on the Reciprocators (chapter 10) are valid for both the long- and the short-term countries in this cluster.

ANNEXES

A

Annex 1: List of countries

COUNTRY	METHOD	CHAPTER	PAGES
Africa	Reciprocator	10	40, 55, 104, 107, 160
Albania	Reciprocator	10	104
Angola	Reciprocator [23]	10	104
Argentina	Reciprocator	10	104
Australia	Competitor	6	40, 48, 53, 55, 152, 155
Austria	Organiser	7	41, 69, 152
Bangladesh	Reciprocator [23]	10	104
Belgium	Diplomat	9	15, 42, 51, 52, 88 – 92, 152
Bhutan	Marathonian	11	118
Brazil	Reciprocator	10	104
Bulgaria	Reciprocator	10	104
Burkina Faso	Reciprocator [23]	10	104
Canada	Competitor	6	55, 152
Cape Verde	Reciprocator	10	104
Chile	Reciprocator	10	104
China	Marathonian	11	39, 114 – 126, 143, 152, 157, 158
Colombia	Reciprocator	10	104
Costa Rica	Reciprocator	10	104
Croatia	Reciprocator	10	104
Czech Republic	Organiser	7	41, 69, 152
Denmark	Connected	8	80, 82, 152
Dominican Republic	Marathonian	11	118
Ecuador	Reciprocator	10	104
Egypt	Reciprocator	10	104
El Salvador	Reciprocator	10	104
Estonia	Connected	8	80
Ethiopia	Reciprocator	10	104
Fiji	Marathonian	11	118
Finland	Connected	8	80, 152
France	Diplomat	9	15, 42, 52, 70, 88 – 98, 152, 159
Germany	Organiser	7	3, 41, 53, 66 – 71, 152
Ghana	Reciprocator	10	104

[23] These countries have a score of 50 on the dimension of Uncertainty Avoidance. We decided to classify them as Reciprocators but you will also find a Marathonian mindset there.

Greece	Reciprocator	10	104
Guatemala	Reciprocator	10	104, 152
Honduras	Reciprocator	10	104
Hong Kong	Marathonian	11	118, 143, 152
Hungary	Organiser	7	69, 152
Iceland	Connected	8	80
India	Marathonian	11	118, 152
Indonesia	Marathonian	11	108, 118
Iran	Reciprocator	10	104
Iraq	Reciprocator	10	104
Ireland	Competitor	6	55, 152
Israel	Organiser	7	69
Italy (North)	Diplomat	9	92, 152, 167
Jamaica	Marathonian	11	118
Japan	Craftsman	12	45, 130–139, 148, 152, 158, 160
Jordan	Reciprocator [23]	10	104
Kenya	Reciprocator	10	104
Kuwait	Reciprocator	10	104
Latvia	Connected	8	80
Lebanon	Reciprocator	10	104
Libya	Reciprocator	10	104
Lithuania	Connected	8	80
Luxembourg	Organiser	7	69, 152, 167
Malawi	Reciprocator	10	104
Malaysia	Marathonian	11	118, 152
Malta	Diplomat	9	92
Mexico	Reciprocator	10	104, 105
Middle East (general)	Reciprocator	10	104, 142, 160
Morocco	Reciprocator	10	104, 105, 106
Mozambique	Reciprocator	10	104
Namibia	Marathonian	11	118
Nepal	Marathonian	11	118
Netherlands	Connected	8	14, 42, 80, 81, 142, 143, 152
New Zealand	Competitor	6	40, 55, 152
Nigeria	Reciprocator [23]	10	104
Norway	Connected	8	80, 152
Pakistan	Reciprocator	10	104
Panama	Reciprocator	10	104
Peru	Reciprocator	10	104
Philippines	Marathonian	11	118
Poland	Diplomat	9	92, 152

Portugal	Reciprocator	10	104, 152
Romania	Reciprocator	10	104
Russia	Reciprocator	10	102, 104, 152, 155
Saudi Arabia	Reciprocator	10	104
Senegal	Reciprocator [23]	10	104
Serbia	Reciprocator	10	104
Sierra Leone	Reciprocator	10	104
Singapore	Marathonian	11	118, 152
Slovakia	Reciprocator	10	104
Slovenia	Reciprocator	10	104
South Africa (white)	Competitor	6	55, 107
South Korea	Reciprocator	10	104
Spain	Diplomat	9	42, 92, 152
Sri Lanka	Marathonian	11	118
Suriname	Reciprocator	10	104
Sweden	Connected	8	80, 152
Switzerland (German)	Organiser	7	41, 69, 152
Switzerland (Fr + It)	Diplomat	9	92, 152
Syria	Reciprocator [23]	10	104
Taiwan	Reciprocator	10	104
Tanzania	Reciprocator	10	104
Thailand	Reciprocator [23]	10	104, 152
Trinidad & Tobago	Reciprocator	10	104
Turkey	Reciprocator	10	104, 152
United Arab Emirates	Reciprocator	10	104
United Kingdom	Competitor	6	40, 48 – 56, 90, 152, 167
U.S.A.	Competitor	6	39, 55, 57, 59, 93, 152
Uruguay	Reciprocator	10	104
Venezuela	Reciprocator	10	104
Vietnam	Marathonian	11	118
Zambia	Reciprocator	10	104
Zimbabwe	Reciprocator	10	104, 107

Annex 2: Biographies

Jean-Pierre's bio

Jean-Pierre is French-Belgian, and at a very young age he founded his own company selling copy paper.

At the age of 32, he sold the company and started to work for the French paper mill Clairefontaine. He rose through the ranks quickly and was in charge of international sales for more than 30 years. During his career, he negotiated commercial deals in more than 40 countries around the world.

Jean-Pierre has lived in Brussels, London and Paris, and at the age of 58, he decided to dedicate himself to transmitting his knowledge to others. In 2013, he wrote his first book: 'Négociation Internationale, L'entretien de vente en B to B', published in French by Edipro. He now dedicates his life to training managers who work and negotiate in an international environment.

Marc's bio

Marc is Flemish-Belgian, holds a SLOAN MSc in Leadership and Strategy from London Business School and a Master's Degree in Engineering from KIH de Nayer in Belgium. He has lived in Belgium, Luxembourg, Italy and the UK, has travelled extensively both professionally and for leisure, and is fluent in 5 languages.

Throughout his career, Marc occupied several senior international positions in Operations, Sales and Marketing, and General Management.

Marc founded Imajine Sàrl, a specialist consultancy in Intercultural Management and Organisational Culture and Strategy.

He is co-founder of 'The House Intercultural Competency Development', a non-profit organisation through which he contributes his skills and knowhow to help integration of refugees and migrant workers in Luxembourg.

Marc is a board member of several international organisations.

Both Jean-Pierre and Marc are associate partners of Hofstede Insights.
jeanpierre.coene@hofstede-insights.com I marc.jacobs@hofstede-insights.com

Printed in Poland
by Amazon Fulfillment
Poland Sp. z o.o., Wrocław

49098977R00100